PELICAN

A227

OUR LANGUAGE

SIMEON POTTER

Our Language

SIMEON POTTER

'. . . the language which so many love
and so few know how to use.'
R. W. CHAPMAN
Last S.P.E. Tract, 1948

PENGUIN BOOKS
BALTIMORE · MARYLAND

Penguin Books Ltd, Harmondsworth, Middlesex
U.S.A.: Penguin Books Inc., 3300 Clipper Mill Road, Baltimore 11, Md
AUSTRALIA: Penguin Books Pty Ltd, 762 Whitehorse Road,
Mitcham, Victoria

—

First published 1950
Reprinted 1951, 1953, 1954, 1956, 1957, 1959
Reprinted with revised bibliography 1961
Reprinted 1963

—

Made and printed in Great Britain
by William Clowes and Sons Ltd
London and Beccles
Set in Monotype Bembo

Contents

24254

Acknowledgement

I have much pleasure in acknowledging my in-
debtedness to friends and colleagues in the University of Liverpool who have been so good as to
discuss with me many of the views expressed in the
following pages and, more particularly, I should
like to avail myself of this opportunity of expressing
thanks to Professor G. L. Brook of the University
of Manchester who kindly read the book in typescript and offered valuable criticisms.

S. P.

CHAPTER I

Introductory

WE cannot know too much about the language we speak every day of our lives. Most of us, it is true, can get along fairly well without knowing very much about our language and without ever taking the trouble to open a volume of *The Oxford English Dictionary*. But knowledge is power. The power of rightly chosen words is very great, whether those words are intended to inform, to entertain, or to move. English is rapidly becoming a cosmopolitan means of communication and it is now being studied by numerous well-trained investigators on both sides of the Atlantic. It is highly exhilarating to contemplate the progress made in the study of English since the opening years of this century, when Henry Bradley of Oxford and Otto Jespersen of Copenhagen were writing those admirable introductions which have become classics of their kind: *The Making of English* and *Growth and Structure of the English Language*. To men like Bradley and Jespersen we all owe much, both for their tangible contributions to learning and for that new spirit of enterprise and adventure with which they have imbued English studies. That assertion, too often repeated, that Englishmen are not really interested in their own language, is no longer valid. At last we English are showing an awakened interest in our mother tongue as something living and changing and amenable to our corporate will. This we see in many differing spheres: in national and local government, in business and journalism, in film and radio, in school and university. Let us all join freely

in the quest and let us share gladly in that intellectual joy of
linguistic exploration which is ours for the seeking every day
of our lives.

Our language belongs to the great Indo-European family,
and it is therefore related to most of the other languages of
Europe and Western Asia from India to Iceland, and to this
vast region we must now add Australia and New Zealand on
the east, North and South America on the west, and parts of
Africa on the south. These languages, nearly or distantly related, all derive and descend from that parent language (called
Indo-European, Indo-Germanic, or Aryan) which was spoken
five thousand years ago by nomads living in the plains of what
is now the Ukraine and Southern Russia. Their starting-point
or first home is not readily ascertainable. Recently discovered
records of Tokharian and Hittite promise to tell us, in the not
distant future, something more than we already know about
these ancestors of ours. From 6000 to 4000 B.C. settled life in
cities had certainly begun in the river valleys of the Euphrates
and the Indus. But perhaps there never was a time when men
and women speaking Proto-Indo-European lived as one community within a definable geographical region. We may
imagine them in the neolithic period wandering about over
the Great Lowland Plain from the Rhine to the Aral Sea, or,
restricting the picture a little, from the Vistula to the Dnieper.
We may fairly regard our ancestral home as a much-extended
Lithuania, that medieval Lithuania which, in fact, reached
from the Baltic across the Ukraine to the lower waters of the
Dnieper. At once we may be reminded that of all the living
languages of Europe Lithuanian is the most archaic, preserving
in its structural pattern the primitive features of Indo-European most faithfully. That is why the comparative philologist
is as much interested in Modern Lithuanian as he is, say, in
Sanskrit or Ancient Greek. Hindi and Modern Greek have
changed so much more rapidly than Lithuanian, spoken by a
people whose homes were shut off for many centuries from

the outside world by primeval forests and impassable marshes. Lithuanian still preserves seven case-forms in its nouns, four tenses and four moods in its verbs, an elaborate series of participles and a highly involved system of inflexions. The distinguished nineteenth-century philologist August Schleicher (1821–68), of the University of Prague, used to spend his summer vacations talking to Lithuanian farmers and recording songs and tales from their lips. He tried hard to reconstruct Indo-European on the basis of Sanskrit for the consonants, Greek for the vowels, and Lithuanian for the inflexions. He had the greatest difficulty, as he himself confessed, with the links or connecting words. Nevertheless, with more zeal than discretion, Schleicher published his nine-line fable of the Sheep and the Horses, *Avis akvasas ka*, in what he conceived to be the 'Aryan primal speech'. The attempt was laudable but temerarious, and it was soon criticized by the *Junggrammatiker*, or Neogrammarians, Brugmann, Osthoff, Paul, Delbrück, and others. Most 'comparatists' to-day, I suppose, would write * *oụis eku̯ōs que* as the most likely forms for 'sheep and horses' in Proto-Indo-European, and they would follow convention by marking the phrase with a star to denote that the forms are hypothetical and that they merely represent assumed forms which may have to be modified later in the light of new knowledge. Yet Schleicher's methods were sound. He proceeded from the known to the unknown, and by talking with Lithuanians he was able to acquire a feeling for a more highly inflected language than his native German and to gain a deeper insight into the earlier stages of Indo-European than most of his contemporaries.

Because Indo-European was an inflected language, word order was free and the division of the sentence into subject and predicate was not so clearly marked. Let us take a simple illustration from Latin. I can say in Latin *Taurus puerum fugavit*, 'The bull chased the boy', and *Taurum puer fugavit*, 'The boy chased the bull', without changing the order of the two substantives, but by varying their inflexions. Or, again, I can vary the word order in either sentence and achieve slightly different shades of emphasis which would be best shown in Modern English by intonation: *Taurus puerum fugavit, Puerum taurus fugavit, Taurus fugavit puerum, Puerum fugavit taurus, Fugavit taurus puerum, Fugavit puerum taurus,* and so on. In Old English I can do this also to a limited extent, but I cannot do it in Modern English without ambiguity. The poet may be willing to run this risk. So, for example, Gray wrote in his *Elegy* –

> And all the air a solemn stillness holds

– and the more thoughtful reader may well wonder whether *air* or *stillness* is the subject, while realizing that the meaning is little affected either way.

From Indo-European to Modern English by way of Common Germanic, West Germanic, Anglo-Frisian, Old English and Middle English, our language has shown a gradual process of simplification and of the breaking down of inflexions. The development has been, for the most part, in one direction all the time: from *synthesis* to *analysis*. There have been both gain and loss. We need not assume too readily with Jespersen that this analytic process has meant unqualified *progress in language* or that our forebears of five, four, and three thousand years ago were less gifted linguistically than we. Think what linguistic alertness and precision are required of those speakers who wield an elaborate system of inflexions effectively and faultlessly! The language of twentieth-century London and New York may become a very fine and delicate instrument in the hands of accomplished masters, but its qualities and potentialities are different from those of, let us say, Periclean Greek. How much Sir Walter Scott regretted that he knew so little Greek! As Gilbert Murray has so well said (in *Greek Studies*), the Greeks had 'built up a language amazingly capable of expressing the various requirements of the human mind: the precision of prose, the magic and passion of poetry, the combination of exactitude and far-flung questioning that constitutes philosophy, the jests refined or ribald that make men laugh two thousand years after. Can one see by what efforts or what accidents this came about; or what actual phenomena of language have led to this strange power? One point seems to be clear, that it depends on a richness of inflexions which enables a speaker to vary greatly the order of his words in the sentence and thus to capture whole territories of emphasis and suggestion that are barred out to the uninflected languages.'

Classical Greek and Common Germanic were roughly contemporaneous and they were alike descended from parent Indo-European. Without mixing metaphors unduly, it may be said that a family has branches and that branches have divisions. The Indo-European family had eight branches of which Greek and Germanic were two, the other six being Indo-Iranian, Armenian, Albanian, Latin, Celtic, and Balto-Slavonic. Germanic (also called Teutonic or Gothonic) later showed three geographical divisions: East Germanic (Burgundian, Vandal, and Gothic); North Germanic (Norwegian, Icelandic, Swedish, and Danish); and West Germanic (German, Dutch, Flemish, Frisian, and English).

When Tacitus wrote that well-known description of the Germanic nations and their institutions called *Germania* in the first century after Christ, those nations were still on the move and that tripartite linguistic division into East, North, and West was in progress. Germania extended from Scandinavia in the north to the Ore Mountains in the south and from the Rhine in the west to the Vistula in the east. No Primitive Germanic writing of any kind is extant and the forms of words assumed for that language are just as hypothetical as those postulated for Indo-European. In our search for the earliest of all Germanic recorded forms we must go north to the runic inscriptions of Scandinavia, the most ancient of which, according to Otto von Friesen, date from the third century. In order to find the most ancient literary records, however, we must look to East Germanic, to the Biblical translations of Wulfila (311–83), Bishop of the Visigoths, who, to escape persecution, led his congregation in the year 348 across the Danube into the Roman province of Lower Moesia, now Bulgaria. Bishop Wulfila continued to lead his people in their new home for a third of a century and during that time he translated the greater part of the Bible into Gothic. This translation was used and revised after his death and some parts have survived from each of the Gospels and from the thirteen Pauline epistles, as well as fragments of Ezra and Nehemiah and a few pages of the *Skeireins* or Commentary. Gothic was still spoken in the seventeenth century in the Crimea, and we know something about this Crimean Gothic because some sixty words of it were noted by a Fleming named Ogier Ghislain van Busbecq, Charles V's envoy from the Low Countries to Constantinople, and published by him in Paris in 1589. It is easy to see why Gothic is valued so highly by the advanced student of English. Wulfila's Bible is the oldest Germanic document, three centuries older than anything in Old English and four centuries older than anything in Old High German. It is the nearest thing to Common Germanic. Without it the 'Anglicist' would be at a yet greater disadvantage than he is already as compared with advanced students of French, Spanish, and Italian who have their Common Italic or Romanic in the form of Latin with its superabundant testimony preserved in the most extensive literature of antiquity.

What proportion of words in present-day English can be traced back with a fair measure of certainty to Indo-European? To this apparently simple question there is no ready answer. Even if we eliminate all those words which, after a little thought, most of us would recognize as non-Indo-European – such words, I mean, as *cherub* and *seraph* from Hebrew, *zenith* and *nadir* from Arabic, *coffee* and *kiosk* from Turkish, and *bamboo* and *sago* from Malay – we are left with many forms whose ulterior etymology is obscure and whose geographical range is surprisingly limited. As we shall see in a later chapter, new expressions may appear overnight as if coming from nowhere. These *ex nihilo* forms may be the deliberate creations of one man or of one social group or of a whole community. Words denoting the closest family relationships, *father* and *mother*, *brother* and *sister*, *son* and *daughter* (but not *husband* and *wife*) go back to the parent language, as we should expect. So, too, do the names of parts of the human body, like *arm*, *ear*, *eye*, *tooth*, *heart*, *foot*, *nail*, and the numerals from *one* to *ten*; *night*, *star*, *dew*, *fire*, *snow*, *thunder*, and *wind*; *feather* and *nest*; *beaver*, *cow*, *goat*, *goose*, *hound*, *mouse*, *ox*, *steer*, *sow*, and *wether*; *door*, *timber*, *thatch* (but not *window*); *axle*, *nave*, *wain*, *wheel*, and *yoke*. As we contemplate that most peaceful of all scenes, a flock of sheep grazing on a hillside, we may reasonably surmise that *ewe*, *lamb*, and *sheep* are all three ancient words, 'as old as the hills'. Yet, as C. T. Onions has recently reminded us (in *The Character of England*), *ewe* alone is of Indo-European range, *lamb* is unknown outside Germanic, and *sheep* is limited to West Germanic. The ewes or yowes of Isobel Pagan's song which so haunted the imagination of Robert Burns –

> Ca' the yowes to the knowes,
>   Ca' them where the heather grows,
> Ca' them where the burnie rows,
>   My bonnie dearie

– are very near to Indo-European *ouis* which we encountered earlier in this chapter in the title of August Schleicher's fable. English *lamb* has its counterpart in Swedish and German *Lamm* and Danish and Dutch *lam*, because these four languages are Germanic, but search where we will – French *agneau*, Spanish *cordero*, Italian *agnello*, Russian *baráshek*, Czech *iehně* – we find other roots or etyma outside Germanic. Dutch *schaap* and German *Schaf* are clearly our *sheep*, but in the

Scandinavian languages we find Danish *Faar* and its variants, reminding us that the Faeroes are probably the Sheep Islands.

I have just glanced at the morning newspaper and I have been joyfully reminded of happy ski-ing holidays by an attractive photograph of the *Langlauf* at St Moritz. *Langlauf* is 'long leap', but *leap* meant 'dance' and 'run' rather than 'jump' in older English. This picture shows the winning-post of the famous Swiss cross-country race. It is *-lauf* and not *-laup* because *-p* is subject to a special change known as the Second or High German Sound Shift seen, for example, in German *Schiff* as compared with English *ship*. We think of Dutch *loop* and then of other similar trios in German, Dutch, and English which show a comparable vowel harmony: *Baum – boom – beam* (our *boom*, like so many other naval terms, is from Dutch; the meaning 'tree' is preserved in *hornbeam*): *Auge – oog – eye* (but Scottish *ee*): *Rauch – rook – reek* (meaning 'smoke' – Edinburgh is 'Auld Reekie'): *Hauf*(e) – *hoop* – *heap* (German again shows the Second Sound Shift; Dutch *hoop* lives in English in 'forlorn hope' for 'forlorn heap' or 'troop'), and so on. Dutch is nearer to English than German is, and Frisian is nearer still. The Frisians, who still inhabit parts of the Dutch province of Friesland as well as the islands along the west coast of Schleswig, were the neighbours of the Angles and the Saxons in the fifth century. There are strong reasons for regarding Anglo-Frisian as one language at that time. Procopius mentioned the Frisians among the early settlers of Britain. They were then a great maritime power with a centre at Dorestad near Utrecht and with colonies in Scandinavia.

Of all the tongues descended from Indo-European, English has had most contacts with its kindred near and far. Leaving their continental homes, the English entered a land inhabited by Celts and they have had Celts as their neighbours ever since. With the coming of Christian missionaries they were brought into close contact with those who spoke Latin and, after the Norman Conquest, with those who spoke various forms of a language derived from Latin. To Latin Greek was added with the revival of learning and, later still, by their memorable political association with India, the English lived and worked for nearly two centuries with peoples whose languages were descended from the oldest and most easterly branch of all.

CHAPTER II

Old English

CERTAIN movements or events stand out in the history of English: the settlement in this island of Jutes, Saxons, and Angles in the fifth and sixth centuries; the coming of St Augustine in 597 and the subsequent conversion of England to Latin Christianity; the Scandinavian invasions in the eighth, ninth, and tenth centuries; the Norman Conquest in the eleventh; the revival of learning in the sixteenth; and the migration of English-speaking people to North America, Australasia, and South Africa mainly in the eighteenth and nineteenth centuries.

Of all these movements the first was clearly the most decisive. Our knowledge of it is derived from *The Ecclesiastical History of the English People*, which was written in Latin by the Venerable Bede about 730, nearly three centuries after the first Jutes, Hengist and Horsa, landed at Ebbsfleet in the Isle of Thanet in 449. Bede did not mention the Frisians, as Procopius had done, but he drew a fairly clear picture of the settlement of Britain by these three related 'nations' or tribes: the Jutes who came first and settled in Kent, Southern Hampshire, and the Isle of Wight; the Saxons who afterwards occupied the rest of England south of the Thames, and then the Angles or English, who founded homes in regions north of the Thames. The Jutes came from Jutland, the Saxons from Holstein, and the Angles from Schleswig. Doubtless the Angles took their name from that *angle* or corner of land which juts out slightly into the Southern Baltic between the modern towns of

Schleswig and Flensburg. In both Latin and Common Germanic their name was *Angli*, and this form became *Engle* in Old English by change of stressed vowel or 'front mutation' in much the same way as *man* has the plural *men* or, with a difference of designation, *Frankish* is used side by side with *French*. Before 1000 A.D. *Angelcynn*, 'Angle-race', and after that date *Englaland*, 'land of the Angles', were used to denote collectively the Germanic peoples in Britain: Angles, Saxons, and Jutes alike. No one spoke of Saxon or *Sexisc*, not even King Alfred himself, the great and good King of the West Saxons. From the beginning the language was always *Englisc*.

Nevertheless, the tripartite division of England was naturally reflected in language and dialect. Inasmuch as Jutes, Angles, and Saxons could probably understand one another, we may speak of three inherited dialects rather than of three separate languages, and because the Humber formed an important geographical and linguistic boundary, we may picture the Anglian-speaking region as subdivided into Northumbrian and Southumbrian or Mercian. There were thus four Old English dialects: Northumbrian, Mercian, West Saxon, and Kentish. In literature and culture Northumbrian led in the eighth century, then Mercian for a short period, and, after that, West Saxon. Winchester superseded Wilton as the West Saxon capital and it remained the linguistic centre of England until the time of King Edward the Confessor, who favoured Westminster and London. The immediate effect of the Norman Conquest was to put all the dialects once more on their mettle, but very soon the Midland region excelled. The differences between East and West Midland were sufficiently marked to justify their being regarded as two dialects. West Midland speech, notably that of the cathedral cities of Hereford and Worcester, was the more direct descendant of Old Mercian and it was in the west country that the continuity of English prose and poetry was most apparent. Wulfstan of

Worcester and Giso of Wells were the only two bishops who were still preaching in Old English when King William I died in 1087. By the thirteenth century, however, the East Midland dialect had risen into greater prominence than the West. It was, after all, the dialect of the Court, of the City of London, and of both universities, Oxford and Cambridge. Later it became the dialect of Chaucer, whose English was essentially East Midland with Southern and Kentish peculiarities; of the trilingual Gower; and of Wyclif, too, although he was a Yorkshireman born.

It has been well worth while to complete this general picture of the English dialects, but we must now return to the time of the early settlements. When the first Jutes arrived in Britain in 449 they came to a Celtic-speaking land. A whole generation had passed away since the Romans had left in 410 and we have no evidence as to how many people still spoke and understood Latin. During those three centuries and more, when Britain was a province of the Roman Empire, Latin was spoken in the cities and larger country villas. Many Latin inscriptions have been discovered, which were doubtless composed by army officers and by those more ambitious artisans who scratched *graffiti* on tiles and earthenware. But such inscriptions do not testify to a widespread use of Latin by the native population. Latin did not displace Celtic in Britain as it displaced Celtic across the sea in Gaul. To the English intruders the Celts offered neither friendship nor culture, and little by little the latter were driven westward. The English victory at Deorham (577) separated Wales from Cornwall and that at Chester (613) separated Wales from Cumbria or Cumberland. Many of the Cornish Celts found new homes in Brittany, where Breton or Armorican is still a living language, whereas Cornish died out in the eighteenth century. Welsh, Manx, Erse, and Gaelic are living tongues, though most Welshmen and all Celtic-speaking Manxmen are bilingual. Many English river-names are Celtic: Aire, Avon, Dee, Derwent (Darent,

Dart), Don, Esk (Axe, Exe), Ouse, Severn, Stour, Tees, Thames, Trent, and Wye. Several of these, like Avon, Esk, and Stour, mean just 'water', but some, like Cald(er) 'violent', Cam 'crooked', Dee 'holy', and Dove 'black', are descriptive. Some names of cities and towns are Celtic: London, Dover, Crewe, York, Leeds, Catterick, Penrith, and Carlisle. To a Celtic name Latin-derived *-chester* or *-cester* may have been added: Dorchester, Gloucester, Leicester, Manchester, Rochester, and Winchester. Upon the Old English spoken language, however, Celtic left few marks.

With the arrival of St Augustine and his forty monks, direct contact was resumed with the life and thought of the Mediterranean. England became a home of learning, and especially England north of the Humber. Hild, Abbess of Whitby, of royal descent, was the best educated of all Anglo-Saxon women. In her monastery Cædmon (fl. 680) received the gift of song. Benedict Biscop, founder of the Wearmouth-Jarrow monastery, on several occasions brought manuscripts from Rome, and his pupil, the Venerable Bede, had access to all the sources of knowledge in the west. The light of learning then shone more brightly in Northumbria than anywhere else in Europe and a notable succession of teachers and pupils was led by the illustrious Benedict Biscop, who, as we have just seen, taught Bede of Jarrow, who in his turn taught Ecgbeorht of York, who taught Alcuin of Tours, who taught Hraban of Fulda, who taught Walafrid Strabo of Reichenau. That light was extinguished by the Scandinavian Vikings, who sacked Lindisfarne in 793 and put an end to monastic learning in the north in 870.

King Alfred (871-99), who saved Wessex from a like fate, recalled the glory of northern learning in the famous Preface to his translation of Gregory's *Pastoral Care*, and he invited scholars to Winchester from Mercia and Wales and even from abroad to help him revive learning in the south. Among the documents which probably come to us from King Alfred's own scriptoria are the earlier portions of the *Parker Chronicle* and the Lauderdale manuscript of Orosius's *History of the World*. The former contains, as the annal for 755, a vivid and dramatic description of the skirmish at Merton in Surrey, some thirty years later, in which King Cynewulf was slain. It is by far the oldest historical prose in any Germanic language. Elsewhere in the *Chronicle* the bare annalistic record expands into a true history, especially in the lively and business-like account of the climax of King Alfred's struggle with the Danes in the years from 893 to 897 and, later, in the passionate and almost personal expressions of grief at the degradation of England under King Ethelred II. In the opening chapter of Orosius, King Alfred left the Latin text he was translating and described the voyages of Ohthere and Wulfstan in his own words. Such passages demonstrate clearly that over a thousand years ago writers of English had developed a useful, all-purpose prose medium. Indeed, English was the earliest and most advanced vernacular in Europe, to be rivalled, a century or two later, by the language of the historic and domestic sagas of Iceland.

The more serious student of English will hardly rest content until he has scrutinized some of this older prose for himself. Excellent handbooks by Sweet, Wyatt, Wright, Marckwardt and others, will make his path easy, but the mere extent of the vocabulary, consisting in all of some thirty thousand words, may well intimidate him at first. How can he hope to master such a vast store of words when even Shakespeare used only twenty-five thousand in his plays, when Milton was content with twelve thousand, and when Sir Winston Churchill probably wields a vocabulary of some sixty thousand? The answer is that many thousands of these Old English words are easily recognizable from their modern forms, that many thousands are slightly disguised compounds whose components are distinguishable after a little acquaintance, and that many thousands more are peculiar to the diction of alliterative poetry. A very great part of the vocabulary of the more original prose, four-fifths perhaps, still lives. Out of one hundred words of the account of King Cynewulf's death just mentioned, fourteen have disappeared from the language altogether, three (*atheling*, *mickle*, and *yare*) are archaic or dialectal, but all the other eighty-three are still in daily use, however much meanings, functions, and forms may have been modified.

King Alfred's scribes had acquired the shapes of their letters from runes and from Latin by way of Old Irish. Modern Erse is still written in characters resembling those of Old English manuscripts. To-day it is customary to print Old English in modern letters, dispensing with *j*, *k*, *q*, *v*, and *z*, and adding *æ* (pronounced as in 'hat'), *þ* (as in 'thin') and *ð* (as in 'then'). Having observed special points about the sounds of *c*, *g*, *cg*, *ng*, *f*, *s*, and *þ*, the reader may proceed with confidence, giving to each symbol its phonetic value. He may note that many common words like *bæc* 'back', *bricg* 'bridge', *cin* 'chin', *cuþ* 'couth, known', and *scip* 'ship', are to be pronounced exactly as in Modern English. The vowels of weak inflexional syllables should be given something of their full quality, since that centralization of unstressed sounds to the neutral murmur-vowel [ə], so deplored by Robert Bridges, was only just beginning in Old Northumbrian and did not spread south until after the tenth century. Sentences should be given their normal modern rhythm and intonation: in native words stress has not shifted very much during the last thousand years. As in Common Germanic, so in Old and Modern English, it is fixed on the root syllable even when prefixes and suffixes are added: 'rise, a'rise, a'rising; 'see, fore'see, fore'seeable; 'glad, 'gladly, 'gladden, 'gladness, 'gladsome; 'king, 'kingly, 'kinglike, 'kingdom, 'kingship. It is interesting to observe that shifting stress, as in Indo-European, is also apparent in present-day compounds derived from Latin and Greek. That series of vowel harmonies which goes by the name of gradation, apophony, or ablaut is still to be discerned in such groups of related words as 'telephone, te'lephony, tele'phonic; 'photograph, pho'tography, photo'graphic from Greek; 'family, fa'miliar, famili'arity; 'contemplate, con'templative, contem'plation from Latin.

Old English, as we have seen, was an inflected language, but it was by no means so highly inflected as Greek, Latin, or Gothic. It stood a little more than half way along that linguistic road leading from Indo-European synthesis to Modern English analysis. Word order resembled that of Modern German, but it was not so strict. It conformed to certain patterns, especially in subordinate clauses. Nevertheless, subject and predicate might change places in main clauses with considerable freedom. It has been calculated that subject precedes object in less than half of King Alfred's sentences. The forms of nouns, pronouns, and adjectives showed grammatical relationship, as they do to-day in pronouns alone: 'Him I know', 'Us they have deceived'. Historically 'If you like' and 'If you please' show conjunctive adverb, pronoun dative, and verb, third person singular, present subjunctive: 'If to you it like or please'. Few people are conscious of this as they speak because feeling for word order is stronger than any other feeling, and indeed such everyday expressions have survived because, without becoming ambiguous, they have readily adapted themselves to the prevalent sentence pattern. 'Him evil likes' has become 'He likes evil'. Instead of 'Cold weather likes us not', we say 'We don't like cold weather'. 'Me is loth' has changed to 'I am loth', and, in spite of loud protests from proscriptive grammarians, 'Me was given the book' has become 'I was given the book' by the most natural process in the world.

In so far as distinctive case-endings survived in Old English, many relationships might still be expressed without a preposition. The plain dative, for example, might denote comparison in the Old English equivalent of 'better than I', accompaniment in 'with a troop of friends', instrument in 'he cut it with a knife', location in 'he dwelt in the woods', as well as reception

in 'the book you gave (*to*) *me*'. Many prepositions have come
to denote changed relationships, but the older meanings may
have survived in petrified expressions which are still in daily
use: *of* meaning 'from' in 'John *of* Salisbury'; *at* meaning
'from' in 'received *at* his hand'; *with* meaning 'against' in
'*with*stand'; *mid* meaning 'with' in '*mid*wife'; *to* meaning 'as'
in 'take *to* wife'; *on* meaning 'in a state of' in 'house *on* fire';
and *over* meaning 'during' in 'to stay *over*night'. Prepositions
were still shifting in Middle and in Elizabethan English. Besides 'repent *of* a misdeed' we encounter in Shakespeare both
'repent *at*' and 'repent *for*'. Prepositions are still shifting to-
day and we may sometimes detect uncertainty of usage
between 'averse *from*' and 'averse *to*', and between 'different
from' and 'different *to*', not to mention 'different *than*' which
appears more than once in the pages of H. G. Wells, and which
is fast gaining currency in America.

Although Old English retained a fairly elaborate system of
declensions, three quarters of the substantives followed three
main strong paradigms for masculines, feminines, and neuters.
Five of the nouns of first relationship, *father*, *mother*, *brother*,
sister, and *daughter*, but not *son*, had a whole separate declen-
sion to themselves. The seven mutated plurals of Modern
English—*feet*, *geese*, *teeth*, *men*, *women*, *lice* and *mice*—had
twenty-five counterparts in Old English, including among
them the plurals of *book*, *goat*, and *oak*, which, if they had
developed independently, would have become *beech*, *geat*, and
each, instead of *books*, *goats*, and *oaks*. It is easy to understand
why regularity has prevailed in these forms and it is surely
remarkable that the seven mutated plurals just mentioned
should have resisted the pull of analogy with such obstinacy
throughout the centuries. They are words in frequent use and
they are therefore less prone to change than rarely used words.
Mans has not superseded *men*, but *oaks* has managed to displace
each. Euphony, too, has doubtless played some part. Intelligent children may form their own plurals *gooses* and *tooths*,

but these forms are, after all, longer and uglier than *geese* and *teeth* and they have failed to find favour.

Old English showed weak declensions of both substantives and adjectives, but *oxen* is the only survival of a weak plural, though *brethren* and *children* are later analogous forms. The personal name Hunt is from the weak noun *hunta*, side by side with Hunter from the strong form *huntere*. In the Southern dialect of Middle English weak plurals were considerably extended: *kine* for 'cows' (the only form in the Authorized Version of the Bible); *treen* for 'trees', *worden* for 'words', *honden* for 'hands', *sistren*, *housen*, *lambren*, *ashen*, *peasen*, and many more. It is odd to reflect that our plurals to-day might end in *-en* and not *-s* if the King's English were descended direct from the Southern dialect of Winchester rather than from the East Midland dialect of London. There are, after all, no *-s* plurals in literary German. With rare exceptions Old English adjectives had two forms, strong and weak, according to function and position, but the weak forms, still significant in Chaucer, were not preserved beyond the fifteenth century. English has been fortunate in shedding this unprofitable distinction with which Dutch, German, and the Scandinavian languages are still unluckily burdened.

English has likewise been fortunate in shedding grammatical gender. Just as we say *der Fuss*, *die Hand*, and *das Auge* in Modern German, so in Old English *foot* was masculine, *hand* feminine, and *eye* neuter, epicene, or common. All nouns were placed into one of these three inherited categories which were not primarily associated with sex. *Woman*, *quean*, and *wife* were synonymous in Old English, all three meaning 'woman', but they were masculine, feminine, and neuter respectively. *Horse*, *sheep*, and *maiden* were all neuter. *Earth*, 'Mother Earth', was feminine, but *land* was neuter. *Sun* was feminine, but *moon*, strangely enough, masculine. *Day* was masculine, but *night* feminine. *Wheat* was masculine, *oats* feminine, and *corn* neuter. Clearly there was no conceivable relationship between grammatical gender and any quality in the object denoted. English has surely gained everything and lost nothing by casting off this useless burden which all the other well-known languages of Europe still bear to their great disadvantage. How, we may ask, has English contrived to cast it off? Is there such a thing as 'the genius of the language'? Can a language be changed by the 'corporate will' of the people who speak it? Perhaps we should look for more specific causes. The gender of an Old English substantive was not always indicated by the form of the ending as it was, with rare exceptions, in Latin and Greek, but rather by the terminations of the adjectives and demonstrative pronouns used in agreement. When these distinguishing terminations were lost in everyday speech, all outward marks of grammatical gender were lost likewise. Weakening of inflexions and loss of gender went on together. In the north where inflexions weakened earlier the marks of gender likewise disappeared first. They were retained in the south as late as the fourteenth century.

In conclusion, it may be pointed out that Old English showed a remarkable capacity for word-formation and for bending old words to new uses. Medicine was expressed by *lǣcecræft* or *lǣcedōm* 'leech-craft' or 'leech-dom', arithmetic by *rīmcræft* 'number-craft', geometry by *eorðcræft*, 'earth-craft', and astronomy by *tungolcræft* 'star-craft'. An astrologer was *tungol-wītega* 'star-prophet'. Fecundity or fertility was well expressed by *wæstmberendnes* 'fruitbearing-ness'. Divinity was rendered by *godcundnes* 'God-kind-ness' and trinity by *þrīnes* 'three-ness'. The word for bishop, borrowed and adapted from Greek, was written *biscop*, but pronounced much as in Modern English: naturally episcopal was *biscoplīc* 'bishoply' and diocese was *biscopscīr* 'bishopshire'. A dean was a *tēoðingealdor* or 'tithing-elder'. The patriarchs and prophets of the Old Testament became *hēahfæderas ond wītegan* 'high-fathers and wise-*men*', whereas the scribes and Pharisees of the Gospels became *bōceras ond sundorhālgan* 'bookers and

CHAPTER III

Scandinavian and French

THE light of learning was extinguished in Northumbria by the Scandinavian Vikings who sacked Lindisfarne in 793, who plundered Bede's own monastery at Jarrow in 794 (Bede having died long before, in 735), and who put an end to monastic schools in the north in 870. All England north and east of Watling Street, leading from London to Chester, fell into their hands and became the Danelaw. Even Wessex was threatened.

The Vikings were cruel and relentless sea-rovers who honoured three virtues above all: courage, loyalty, and generosity. These were the qualities that had been esteemed by the pagans of the Germanic Heroic Age (A.D. 325-575) commemorated in the Old English *Widsith, Waldere, Deor, The Fight at Finnsburg*, and *Beowulf*, the Old High German *Hildebrand*, and, later, in the Old Norse sagas. The Viking Age (A.D. 750-1050) witnessed an extraordinary effusion of vitality among the men, especially the younger landless sons, of Southern Scandinavia and Denmark which impelled them on their daring and enterprising voyages along the sea-coasts of Western Europe and which drove them east to Constantinople and west to Massachusetts. The Danes still inhabited Scania in Southern Sweden. The Vikings consisted of both Norwegians and Danes and they were near akin in both race and language to the Angles, Jutes, Saxons, and Frisians who had preceded them in crossing to Britain. They were related, after all, to Alfred himself, that great Christian King of the West Saxons

(871–99), who bore the brunt of their attacks, winning a victorious peace from the Danish King Guthrum in 886, but leaving the reconquest of the Danelaw to his children, his son Edward the Elder, King of Wessex, and his daughter Æthel- flæd, Lady of the Mercians.

The heart of the Danelaw lay between the Tees and the Welland. It comprised the Kingdom of York, which kept in close touch with the Viking Kingdom of Dublin, and the district of the Five Boroughs, Derby, Nottingham, Lincoln, Leicester, and Stamford. When Eric Bloodaxe, last King of York, was slain on Stainmore in 954, England first became one under Alfred's youngest grandson, King Eadred. Close political unity was achieved later under the Danish King Cnut or Canute (1016–35). In Cnut's day a Danish colony of traders throve in London. Cnut was king not only of England (1016) but also of Denmark (1019) and of Norway (1028). Unfortunately for England, he died at the early age of forty years. We may muse entertainingly on what might have been the course of events had this competent ruler lived and governed until he was twice that age.

The early settlers were Danes. Later they were joined by Norwegians from Ireland, the Isle of Man and the Hebrides, who founded homes in Cumberland and Westmorland, in the western dales of Yorkshire, and in Lancashire and Cheshire. The place-name Normanby, that is, Nor-man-by, derives from Norðmanna býr 'village of the Northmen, Norsemen or Norwegians'. Now Normanby is the name of four villages in Lincolnshire and of three villages in the North Riding. These seven communities, we may surmise, were so named by their neighbours because they were Norwegian settlements in a countryside predominantly Danish. Conversely, Denby and Denaby in the West Riding, from Dena býr 'village of the Danes', like Denby in Derbyshire and Denver in Norfolk, were the names of Danish communities in districts pre- dominantly Norwegian and English. It is no less interesting to observe that there are four villages named Irby in England, *Ira býr* 'village of the Irish, or Norwegians from Ireland'. They are similar in their distribution to the Normanbys, for one is in Cheshire Wirral, one in the North Riding, and two in Lincolnshire. Irby in Wirral has, indeed, its recorded history. Lady Æthelflæd granted land in Wirral to the Irish King Ingemund. Other Scandinavian names in Wirral are Meols, from *melr* 'sand-dune', Thurstaston, from *þorsteins tún* 'Thorstein's farm', Frankby and West Kirby.

When riding across country or when wandering along the lanes you must often have been struck by strange names on signposts. Scandinavian endings are easy to recognize in the names of towns and villages, homesteads, dairy-farms, and pastures. The most distinctive is *-by* 'village', as in Derby and Whitby, but there are many others, like *-beck* 'brook', in Birkbeck and Troutbeck; *-brack*, *-breck*, and *-brick* 'slope', in Haverbrack, Norbreck, and Scarisbrick; *-fell* 'hill', in Scafell and Whinfell; *-garth* 'yard', in Applegarth and Arkengarthdale; *-gill* 'ravine', in Gaisgill and Garrigill; *-keld* 'spring', in Hallikeld and Trinkeld; *-mel* 'sand-dune', in Cartmel and Rathmel; *-rigg* 'ridge', in Crossrigg and Lambrigg; *-scale* 'hut', in Portinscale and Seascale; *-scough* 'wood', in Ayscough and Myerscough; *-skeith* 'racing track', in Hesketh and Wickham Skeith; *-slack* 'shallow valley', in Nettleslack and Witherslack; *-thwaite* 'clearing, paddock', in Bassenthwaite and Braithwaite; and *-toft* 'piece of land, homestead', in Langtoft and Lowestoft. As we ramble up hill and down dale in Cumberland or as we move more swiftly across the plains of Cheshire, we frequently encounter neighbouring villages with Scandinavian, Celtic, and English names – such as Motherby, Penruddock, and Hutton, north of Ullswater; or Helsby, Ince, and Elton, south of the River Mersey – reminding us that these three peoples eventually settled down together, tilled the soil, erected homesteads, drained the marshes, made walls and hedges, built churches and held their market-days.

Many good old Scandinavian words live in names and many, too, are preserved in common speech. Joseph Wright, editor of *The English Dialect Dictionary* (1896–1905), embarked on dialect study with a detailed scrutiny of the speech of his own native village of Windhill in the West Riding, where hundreds of Norse words, unknown in standard English, are heard every day. Some of these ancient words, like *addle* 'to earn' and *ettle* 'to strive', live still in dialect from Leicester to Northumberland. Some are more widely known in proverbs, those succinct expressions of inherited wisdom: 'A bonny bride is soon *buskit* (dressed, prepared) and a short horse is soon *wispit* (bedecked)'; 'A *toom* (empty) purse makes a *blate* (bashful, unenterprising) merchant'; 'Never make *toom rusie* (empty boast or brag)'; 'A *wight* (valiant) man never wanted a weapon'; 'Better sit and rue than *flit* (move house) and rue'; 'Hall *binks* (benches) are sliddery (Great men's favours are precarious)'; 'Oft *ettle* (aim), whiles hit'. Dialectal *dag* is a collateral or variant of 'dew' and to *dag* means 'to drizzle'. *Trigg* means 'true', *store* 'great', *glegg* 'clear-sighted, discerning, clever', *heppen* 'neat, tidy', and *gain* 'direct, handy', as in 'the gainest way'. *Gar* signifies 'to make, do', *laik* 'to play', *lait* 'to seek', *keek in* 'to take a peep', and *red up* 'to make tidy'.

English and Scandinavian forms may sometimes both be heard in standard speech: *no* and *nay*; *from* and *fro* in 'to and fro'; *rear* and *raise*; *shirt* and *skirt*, with their different meanings; *shreech* and *screak*, with mixed forms *shriek* and *screech*; *edge* and *egg* in the sense 'to egg on, incite'.

It almost goes without saying that there are scores of common words in daily use which would be identical in form whether they came from English or Scandinavian: words like *father* and *mother*, *man* and *wife*; *town*, *gate*, *house*, and *room*; *ground*, *land*, *tree*, and *grass*; *life* and *folk*; *summer* and *winter*;

cliff and *dale*. Many verbs are the same, especially simple monosyllabic verbs like *bring*, *come*, *hear*, *meet*, *ride*, *see*, *set*, *sit*, *smile*, *spin*, *stand*, *think*, and *will*; adjectives like *full* and *wise*, and names of colours, *grey*, *green*, and *white*; disjunctive possessives *mine* and *thine* (but not *ours* and *yours*) ; *north* and *west* (but not *south* and *east*) ; and the prepositions *over* and *under*.

The Scandinavians of the Danelaw left their marks on manorial organization, local government, and law. Many legal terms were borrowed by the English quite early. The word *law* is itself Scandinavian and it signifies 'that which is *laid* down', just as English *doom* means 'that which is *placed* or *put*' (the older denotation of 'to do') and Latin-derived *statute* 'that which *stands* or *is fixed*'. So *by-law* is 'village or local law' and an *outlaw* is 'a man outside the law'. Other Scandinavian terms associated with law which have displaced their English counterparts are *husband*, from *húsbóndi* 'householder, one who dwells in, and so manages, a house' irrespective of marriage; *fellow*, from *félagi* 'one who lays down *fé* or money', and so 'partner, shareholder'; *grith* 'guaranteed security, sanctuary, asylum'; *husting*, from *hús þing* originally 'house assembly'; *wapentakes*, into which the *ridings* or 'thirdings, third parts' of Yorkshire and Lincolnshire were divided instead of 'hundreds' or 'sokes'.

Names of certain parts of the human body also come from Scandinavian: *calf*, *leg*, *skin*, and *skull*. Among names of animals we find *bull*, *kid*, and *rein(deer)*. Other substantives include *anger*, *axle*, *band*, *bank*, *birth*, *boon*, *booth*, *brink*, *crook*, *dirt*, *down* (feathers), *dregs*, *egg*, *gait*, *gap*, *girth*, *hap*, *haven*, *keel*, *knife*, *link*, *loan*, *mire*, *race* (act of running), *reef* (of sail), *rift*, *root*, *scab*, *scales*, *score*, *scrap*, *seat*, *skill*, *sky*, *slaughter*, *snare*, *stack*, *steak*, *swain*, *thrift*, *tidings*, *trust*, *want*, and *window*.

Like *scant*, (a)*thwart*, and dialectal *wight*, *want* preserves the neuter form in *-t* of the adjective which is characteristic of the Scandinavian languages. *Want* is now noun and verb and as verb its domain is ever increasing. In such expressions as 'I want to know more about this' *want* is clearly superseding *will*, *wish*, *need*, and *should like* from Old English and *desire* from Latin through French.

Other adjectives besides *scant* are *awkward*, *flat*, *happy*, *ill*, *loose*, *low*, *meek*, *muggy*, *odd*, *rotten*, *rugged*, *seemly*, *sly*, *tight*, *ugly*, *weak*, and *wrong*; and other verbs besides *want* are *call*, *cast*, *clasp*, *clip*, *cow*, *crave*, *crawl*, *cut*, *drown*, *die*, *droop*, *egg* (on), *flit*, *gape*, *gasp*, *glitter*, *lift*, *lug*, *nag*, *rake*, *rid*, *rive*, *scare*, *scout* (an idea), *scowl*, *skulk*, *snub*, *sprint*, *take*, *thrive*, and *thrust*; the causative verbs *bait* 'to make bite' and *raise* 'to make rise'; the reflexive verb *bask* 'to bathe oneself'; the compound verb *ransack*; as well as verbs ending in -*en* and -*le*, like *batten* and *happen*, *dangle*, *dazzle*, and *kindle*. We now say 'take' and not *nim*, for *taka* has ousted Old English *niman*, though *nim* in the sense of 'steal' was still common in the colloquial speech of the seventeenth century. *Cast*, having taken the place of *warp*, is itself being superseded by *throw*. *Cut* has caused *carve* and *die* has caused *starve* to have their meanings restricted.

Other prepositions besides *fro* and *thwart* are *till* and *until* (from *und* 'as far as' +*til* 'to'). Further, the pronouns *they*, *their* (from the genitive *þeira* 'of them') and *them* and the pronominal adjectives *both* and *same* have also come into our language from Scandinavian.

Hitherto English had lacked an adequate system of pronouns and ambiguities were multiplied in Middle English when *hē* 'he', *hēo* 'she', and Anglian *hēo* 'they' (West Saxon *hīe*, *hī*, *hȳ*) became identical in pronunciation. Even in the lively verse-tale of *Havelok*, in which the new feminine pronouns *she* and *sho* are in full use, *he* may mean 'he' or 'they', and the listener or reader must gather the meaning from the context. That is why Middle English adopted and adapted these structural words from Scandinavian to supply its needs. Then, as now, intelligibility was a strong determining factor. When men find that their words are imperfectly apprehended they naturally modify their speech and they deliberately prefer the unambiguous form. Between English and Scandinavians there was a merging, an interchange of forms. Two forms for one thing may have been current in a village for many generations. To-day we say *sister* from Old Norse *systir* and not *swester* from Old English *sweostor*, we say *egg* and not *ey*, *weak* and not *woak*, *window* (Old Norse *vindauga* 'wind eye') and not *eye-thurl* or *eye-thril* (Old English *ēagþyrel* 'eye hole'). We say *take them* and not *nim em*, and *they are* and not *he sind*. We no longer use *unfair* in the sense of *ugly* (Old Norse *uggligr* 'to be dreaded') or *unright* in the sense of *wrong* (Old Norse *wrangr* 'twisted, awry').

Scandinavian also left its mark upon our language in its extensive use of verbs with adverb-prepositions of the type *take up, down, in, out, off, on, from*, and *to*. These forms were commonly used in Middle and Elizabethan English, but they were later scorned by the classicists and condemned outright by Dr Johnson. They have multiplied exceedingly in recent years, especially in America.

No less far-reaching was the influence of Scandinavian upon the inflexional endings of English in hastening that wearing away and levelling of grammatical forms which gradually spread from north to south. It was, after all, a salutary influence. The gain was greater than the loss. There was a gain in directness, in clarity, and in strength.

Old Norse was spoken in England as a separate tongue long after the death of King Cnut in 1035. Indeed, it was spoken in remote parts of Scotland until the seventeenth century. But the period of greatest influence was already past when Cnut died and within seven years King Edward the Confessor, who had been reared in France, sat on the English throne. The linguistic climate was changed. Scandinavian receded before Norman French.

For the first one and a half centuries the main influence came from Normandy and Nor-man-d-y, or 'Northmen's land', was just another Danelaw carved out of France. The Normans

2

were mostly Norsemen who had completely shed their Scandinavian speech. They were the great-grandchildren of the fiord who had retained all the Viking energy in colonization and in war, but who had become converts to Latin culture. It was in accordance with the terms of the Treaty of St Clair-sur-Epte in 912 that Hrolf the Ganger, or Rollo the Rover, ancestor of William the Conqueror, was awarded Normandy by the weak French king at Paris, Charles the Simple. With amazing adaptability, Rollo's Vikings created one of the most highly organized states in the world and it was by this state that England was conquered. William took a chance when he landed at Pevensey in 1066 and by clever stratagem won the Battle of Hastings. For the next three centuries and more, all the kings of England spoke French, and, with the exception of Henry I, no king of England until Edward IV (1461–83) sought a wife in England. Henry Bolingbroke (1399–1413), who took the throne one year before Chaucer died, was the first king after the Norman Conquest whose mother tongue was English. Even Edward III (1327–77), victor of Crécy and Poitiers, whom we picture as so very English in character, spoke French more fluently than he spoke the language of his subjects.

Of all the Anglo-Saxon bishops who held office when William arrived, only two outlived him: Wulfstan of Worcester and Giso of Wells. They were pastors in the West Country where men's lives were least affected by foreign influences. They continued to address their congregations in Old English, like Samson (1135–1211), Abbot of Bury St Edmunds in East Anglia, who, according to Jocelin de Brakelond, his biographer, was able to express himself eloquently in both Latin and French, but who preached to the people of Bury in the dialect of Norfolk where he had been born and bred. Not far away at Peterborough the scribes had continued to write their Chronicle in English until the end of Stephen's inglorious reign (1154).

Abbot Samson of Bury, whom Carlyle later idealized in *Past and Present*, was exceptional. Most of his fellow abbots were able to preach in Latin and French only, and many of them held offices on both sides of the Channel. John of Salisbury, that twelfth-century Erasmus, who was Becket's friend and who witnessed the 'murder in the cathedral' on December 29, 1170, died as Bishop of Chartres. The nobility, ecclesiastical and lay, was French-speaking. *Vor bote a man conne frenss me telþ of him lute* 'Unless a man know French, one counts of him little', wrote the chronicler who goes by the name of Robert of Gloucester. Unlike Scandinavian, French became the language of a superior social class. With the extension of Henry II's Angevin Empire (1154–89) to the Pyrenees, other French dialects influenced English too. To-day we have *chase, guardian, guarantee, gage* (as in 'throw down a gage'), and *regard* from Central French side by side with *catch, warden, warrant, wage,* and *reward* from Norman French. King John lost Normandy in 1204 and, with the rise into power of the Capetian Kings of Paris, Central French influence preponderated.

Meantime the language of King Alfred was transformed but its life was at no time in jeopardy. For three centuries, indeed, the literature of England was trilingual – English, Latin, and French – and we must likewise make ourselves trilingual if we would study it seriously. We may regard October 1362, just three centuries less four years after the Battle of Hastings, as the climacteric or turning-point, for it was in that month that Parliament was first opened in English and when the Statute of Pleading was enacted whereby all court proceedings were to be henceforth conducted in English though 'enrolled in Latin'. Law French, it is true, persisted for many years longer. Cromwell tried hard to break it, but it was finally abolished by Act of Parliament in 1731. Law French is still retained in the form of the royal assent (*Le roi le veult*) or refusal (*Le roi s'avisera*) to a Bill in Parliament. We see French in the Royal Arms (*Dieu et mon droit*): for example, at the head of *The Times* newspaper; we find French in the crest of the Garter (*Honi soit qui mal y pense*), in the language of heraldry, in expressions like *congé d'élire*, giving permission to a cathedral chapter to fill a vacant see by election, and in *oyez* 'give hearing', often pronounced *O yes*, the court crier's call for silence deriving ultimately from Latin *audiātis*. We still have R.S.V.P. (*Répondez s'il vous plaît*) printed on our invitation cards and we still use Messrs (for *Messieurs*) in everyday correspondence.

Geoffrey Chaucer was probably a young man of twenty-two when the Statute of Pleading was passed. Later in life he spoke French and Italian, but he wrote his great poems in English. Nevertheless he assumed an acquaintance with French in his hearers and readers. It has been computed that he used just over eight thousand words in his writings, of which a little over four thousand were of Romance origin. In this, as in so many other ways, he anticipated the future. Our present-day vocabulary is approximately half Germanic (English and Scandinavian) and half Romance (French and Latin). The two types are strangely blended. Whereas our titles of nobility, *prince, peer, duke, duchess, marquis, marchioness, viscount, viscountess,* and *baron* are French, the names of the highest rulers, *King* and *Queen*, are English. So too are *lord* and *lady* and also *earl*, although the earl's wife is a *countess*. The French words *people* and *nation* have superseded the Old English *þēod* and Middle English *thede*, which was still current in the fifteenth century but which now survives only in *Thetford* 'people's or public ford', the names of places in Cambridgeshire and Norfolk. *Parliament*, 'speaking, conference', is French, but *Speaker*, the title of the First Commoner, is English. *Shire* is English and we speak of 'a man from the shires', but *county* has been used side by side with it from the thirteenth century. *Town, hamlet, hall, house,* and *home* are English, but *city, village, palace, mansion, residence,* and *domicile* are French. French, too, are *chamber* and *apartment*, whereas *room* and *bower* are English.

Law, as we have seen, is Scandinavian; *right* and *righteousness* from *right-wise-ness* are English; but *justice*, *just*, *judge*, *iury*, and *juridical* are all French. So too are *court*, *assize*, *prison*, *bill*, *act*, *council*, *tax*, *custom*, *mayor*, *manor*, *chattel*, *money*, and *rent*, which all came into our language before the close of the thirteenth century.

Readers of Scott's *Ivanhoe* will remember the conversation between the Saxon thralls Wamba and Gurth in the first chapter, where stress is laid on the fact that the names of the live animals *ox*, *swine*, and *calf* are English, whereas those of the cooked meats *beef*, *pork*, and *veal* are French. Wilfred of Ivanhoe served with Richard Cœur de Lion in the third crusade and, as John Wallis observed long ago in his *Grammatica Linguae Anglicanae* (1653), it is very doubtful whether these French words had acquired these specialized meanings so soon. Nevertheless the picture would apply to the fourteenth century if not to the twelfth. Gladly we testify to the superiority of French cooking, which is duly demonstrated by such culinary terms as *boil*, *broil*, *fry*, *grill*, *roast*, *souse*, and *toast*. *Breakfast* is English, the less simple *dinner* and *supper* are French. *Hunt* is English, but *chase*, *quarry*, *scent*, and *track* are French. Names of the older crafts are English: *baker*, *fisherman*, *miller*, *saddler*, *builder*, *shepherd*, *shoemaker*, *wainwright*, *weaver*, and *webber*. Those of more elegant occupations are French: *carpenter*, *draper*, *joiner*, *mason*, *painter*, and *tailor*. The names of the commoner parts of the human body are English, but French *face* and *voice* have ousted the native *anleth* and *steven* (Old English *andwlita* and *stefn*).

English and French expressions may have similar denotations but slightly different connotations and associations. Generally the English words are stronger, more physical, and more human. We feel more at ease after getting a *hearty welcome* than after being granted a *cordial reception*. Compare *freedom* with *liberty*, *friendship* with *amity*, *kingship* with *royalty*, *holiness* with *sanctity*, *happiness* with *felicity*, *depth* with *profundity*, and *love* with *charity*. As French words became acclimatized they were liable to acquire English endings. Chaucer spoke of *beauty*, but the epithet *beautiful* was first used by Tyndale. The native suffix *-ly* was added to *court* and *prince* and, later, it became associated with adverbs generally. Similarly *-ship* was used to form new abstract nouns like *companionship*, *courtship*, and *scholarship*. Conversely, the French ending *-able*, taken over ready made in the forms *agreeable*, *tolerable*, and *variable*, was then freely added to the English *bear* to make *bearable*. We may observe the valuable and differing distinctions between *readable* (of style), *legible* (of handwriting), *unutterable* and *ineffable*, *answerable* and *responsible*, *eatable* and *edible*.

In that intermingling and blending of the two languages, which was most active in the fourteenth century, Chaucer's influence was weighty. His personal decision to write only in English was of great moment. Chaucer might have written in three languages, like his contemporary Gower or, for that matter, like his successor Milton. He deliberately preferred to be modern, and he endowed the English language with both flexibility and grace. After Chaucer our language moved from strength to strength in the hands of Tyndale and Shakespeare, Milton and Swift.

CHAPTER IV

The Revival of Learning

WHY is it that so many of our technical terms derive from Greek? Primarily it is because Athens once led the world in art, science, and philosophy and because the Greek language is peculiarly well adapted to supply the need in English for precise and unambiguous terms with no inherited penumbra of meaning. Greek has, too, an unusual capacity for forming compounds by means of an extensive and regular system of suffixes. Moreover, there are historical causes.

Athens reached the height of her power in the time of Pericles (c. 495–429 B.C.). Within the century following, Socrates, Plato, and Aristotle lived and taught. After the decline of Athens much Greek learning was preserved in Latin and much, too, in Arabic, especially scientific treatises on medicine, astronomy, and mathematics. This Arabic learning eventually found its way into Western Europe by circuitous paths through Sicily and Spain, but much was lost until the year 1453, when the capture of Byzantium or Constantinople by the Ottoman Turks dispersed Greek-speaking clerks, who fled to the west. Eminent English scholars, like the Venerable Bede of Jarrow in the eighth century and John of Salisbury in the twelfth, certainly had some knowledge of Greek. They knew some Greek words, but it is doubtful whether they could read Greek with ease. Learning they regarded above all as the instrument of the good life, and, like most other scholars in the Middle Ages, they found in Latin all that they sought. Chaucer was content to derive his knowledge of Greek philosophy almost entirely from Boethius. Petrarch, whom he met in Italy, wept over a manuscript of Homer which he could not read. Boccaccio tried to learn Greek, we are told, without success. In thirteenth-century England, however, there had been two notable exceptions: Robert Grosseteste, the great Bishop of Lincoln, and his yet greater pupil, Roger Bacon, the Doctor Mirabilis. By more than two centuries these men anticipated the revival of Greek learning in England at the hands of William Grocyn and Thomas Linacre. Grocyn was a priest and he taught John Colet, afterwards Dean of St Paul's, who startled his hearers by expounding St Paul's Epistles as living human documents. Linacre, translator of Galen, was a physician and he taught Sir Thomas More Greek at Oxford. Under More's hospitable roof at Chelsea, Erasmus of Rotterdam was always sure of finding a warm welcome, and that cosmopolitan scholar was later induced to serve from 1511 to 1514 as Lady Margaret Reader in Greek at Cambridge. Ever since the days of Linacre and Erasmus, Greek has been taught continuously at Oxford and Cambridge. Other countries too have been no less devoted to classical scholarship, especially Scandinavia and Holland. But Greek scholarship left a far deeper mark on English because Englishmen had already acquired the speech-forming habit of borrowing words freely from other tongues. They were quite prepared to borrow Latin words through French, or Latin words direct; Greek words through Latin by way of French, Greek words through Latin, or Greek words direct. Latin and Greek words found their way into English because they were needed. Further, the boundaries of human knowledge were being rapidly extended and this new knowledge was disseminated for the first time by means of printed books.

The names of the seven liberal arts of the medieval trivium and quadrivium had all been Greek-derived words: grammar, logic, and rhetoric; arithmetic, geometry, astronomy, and music. The word *grammar*, by the way, is interesting. Like *beautiful* and *bearable*, which we were considering in the previous chapter, it is a hybrid. It is made up of elements from different languages. It comes by way of Old French from Latin *ars grammatica*, which is itself a translation of Greek *grammatikḗ téchnē*, 'the art pertaining to literature, letters, or written marks'. To the Greek root *gram(m)-* is added the Latin suffix *-ārius* in this particular case, although the usual Latin-derived suffixes are *-ous*, *-an*, and *-al*, as in *analogous*, *amphibian*, and *orchestral*. In his *Treatise on the Astrolabe* Chaucer used and explained Greek terms for the benefit of 'little Lewis', his 'dear son', and he made frequent references to both astronomy and astrology elsewhere in his works, which were copied and studied assiduously by his admirers throughout the fifteenth century. The way was thus well prepared for the importation of words like *drama*, first recorded in 1515, and of terms relating to the drama: *theatre* and *amphitheatre*; *comedy* and *tragedy*; *catastrophe, climax, episode, scene, dialogue, prologue,* and *epilogue*.

The capacity for forming compound words may be illustrated from the Greek verb *poiéō* 'I make'. From this verbal form derives *poíēma* 'something made or created, an object of making', *poíēsis* 'the process of making', *poiētéos* verbal adjective 'to be made', *poiētikós* 'able or disposed to make', and *poiētḗs* 'maker'. The *poet*, then, like the *scop* of Old English (related to *scieppan* 'to shape') and the *makere* of Middle English, is, first and foremost, the creator. *Poesy*, now somewhat archaic, was the earlier form in Tudor English; *poem* is unrecorded before the middle of the sixteenth century. From *poetic* was formed *poetical* by the addition of an extra Latin suffix in *-al*. As for *poetry* itself, it was first used by Chaucer in the form *poetrie* from late Latin *poetria*.

Another illustration is afforded by the compounds and derivatives in Modern English of Greek *gignṓskō* 'I get to know' and related *gnôsis* 'knowledge, wisdom'. *Gnosis* is applied in English to that higher, spiritual wisdom claimed by the *gnostics*. The *agnostics*, on the other hand, claim that nothing is or can be known about God or a future life, and that knowledge is limited to material phenomena. When a physician identifies a disease from its symptoms he makes a *diagnosis*, and when he expresses his expert opinion on its probable future course he offers a *prognosis*. Anyone may venture to *prognosticate*, foretell or predict what may happen in certain circumstances. A man's cast of countenance is his *physiognomy*, but, more strictly, this implies 'the art of getting to know a man's *phúsis* or nature' from his face. The *gnomon* of a sundial is the indicator by which we 'get to know' the hour marked.

Scores of Greek words have made themselves so much at home that it is only by an effort that we recall their earlier significations. An *acrobat* is, etymologically, a 'point-walker, one who walks on tiptoe'; an *athlete* is a 'contestant for an *athlon* or prize'; and the *protagonist* is the 'first actor' of three, the *deuteragonist* and the *tritagonist* being the second and third. An *asylum* is any 'place exempt from *súlē*, or the right of seizure, and so refuge or sanctuary'; an *atom* is something 'uncut or indivisible' and has come to mean an 'individual person' in Modern Greek; a *catastrophe* is a 'down turn', a *character* an 'engraving', a *crisis* a selection or judgement, a *comma* something 'struck or cut', especially the 'stamp or impression on a coin'. *Panic* is short for 'panic fear', that is, 'groundless fear', such sudden terror being inflicted upon us by the god Pan. A *cycle* is merely a 'circle' and an *encyclopedia* is a 'child-training or education in a circle'. If you examine the prospectus of subjects taught in any European or American university, technical college, or technological institute, you will find that Greek-derived names preponderate. *The Nomenclature of Disease*, that important publication which is subject to constant revision by a special committee appointed by the Royal College of Physicians of London, is full of Greek terms, many of which would doubtless have appeared bewildering to Galen and Hippocrates. The present-day forms may not be un-exceptionable on etymological grounds, but they serve their turn. They are useful because they point definitely to one thing or referend and because they are immediately intelligible to specialists throughout the world.

In modern medical usage certain Greek suffixes, like *î-tis* and *-ōsis*, have acquired a new 'slant' in order to meet new needs. The feminine adjectival suffix *-îtis* in Greek corre-sponded to the masculine *-ítēs* which has become *-ite* in Eng-lish in words like *Semite*, *Darwinite*, and *selenite* 'dweller in the moon'. This *-îtis* form was frequently used with the feminine substantive *nósos* 'disease' expressed or understood: *arthrîtis* (*nósos*) 'disease of the joints', *nephrîtis* (*nósos*) 'disease of the kidneys'. Later this suffix was used to denote exclusively those diseases which are characterized by inflammatory condition: *appendicitis* 'inflammation of the vermiform appendix'; *bron-chitis* 'of the mucous membrane of the bronchial tubes'; *con-junctivitis* 'of the inner surface of the eyelids'; *endocarditis* 'of the membranous lining of the heart'; *gingivitis* 'of the gums'; *peritonitis* 'of the serous membrane of the abdomen'; *phlebitis* 'of the veins'; *poliomyelitis* 'of the grey marrow of the spinal chord', popularly known as infantile paralysis. Faceti-ously *-itis* is now fast becoming a living suffix implying 'fever-ish excitement' and it may be attached to any word: *pageantitis* (Rose Macaulay), *motoritis*, *radioitis*, *examinationitis*.

The feminine substantival suffix *-ōsis* meant normal 'state, condition or process', as in *symbiosis* 'a living together (of two dissimilar organisms for purposes of nutrition)' and *meta-morph-osis*, of which Latin *trans-form-ation* is an exact transla-tion, part for part. In medical terminology, however, *-osis* denotes 'disease', as in *halitosis* 'foul breath', *neurosis* 'func-tional disorder of the nerves', *psychosis* 'mental anxiety', and *tuberculosis* 'disease caused by the tubercle bacillus', this last being a hybrid since the first component comes from Latin *tuberculum*, diminutive of *tuber* 'swelling'.

The electricians now speak of *dynatrons* and *kenotrons*; *phanotrons*, *magnetrons*, and *thyratrons*. In the hitherto 'indivisible' *atom* the nuclear physicists now discover *electrons*, *neutrons*, and *protons*, and they proceed to build *cyclotrons* and *synchrotrons*. The last four letters of *electron* (from *electro-* or *electr-ic* + the neuter suffix *-on*) have thus become a new noun-forming suffix. I once heard an unkind critic allude disparagingly to these neologisms as dog-Greek. To a lover of the language of Sophocles and Plato these recent coinages may indeed appear to be Greek debased. More appropriately, perhaps, they might be termed lion-Greek or chameleon-Greek. They are Neo-Hellenic in the genuine Renaissance tradition.

The classical Renaissance of the sixteenth century led to a yet more wholesale importation of Latin words. For a time 'the whole Latin vocabulary became potentially English'. Whereas some words, like *consolation*, *gravity*, *infernal*, *infidel*, *position*, and *solid*, might have come into the language in those forms from either French or Latin, many expressions, like *abacus*, *abecedarium*, *arbitrator*, *ergo*, *executor*, *explicit*, *finis*, *gratis*, *imprimis*, *incipit*, *index*, *item*, *major* and *minor*, *memento*, *memorandum*, *mittimus*, *neuter*, *pauper*, *persecutor*, *proviso*, *simile*, and *videlicet*, were taken straight from Latin without change. Zeal for classical learning led men to reshape French-derived words on Latin models. Good Chaucerian words like *descryve*, *parfit*, and *verdit* were transformed into *describe*, *perfect*, and *verdict*. *Peynture* was changed to *picture*, *avys* to *advice*, and *aventure* to *adventure*. The Biblical idiom *to draw a bow at a venture* (I Kings xxii. 34) preserves the older form, the unstressed *a-* in *at aventure* 'from chance' having been mistaken for an indefinite article. More obscurely, the older form is likewise preserved in the verb *saunter* from French *s'aventurer* 'to hazard oneself, venture, take one's chance'. *Dette* and *doute* were written *debt* and *doubt*, and *vittles* was written *victuals*, but no one took any notice of these spelling changes in speaking. Some such remodelling was likewise undertaken in French when, for example, *captive* was substituted for *caitiff*. Both words are now used in English, but with different meanings.

Some of the new spellings were based on misconceptions. Middle English *iland*, for example, from Old English *īeg* 'isle' + *land*, was erroneously associated with its Romance synonym *isle* from Latin *insula*. So *iland* was written and printed *island*, though no one ever attempted to pronounce the inserted sibilant. *Sissors* from Old French *cisoires* and *sithe* from Old English *sīðe* or *sigðe* both came to be wrongly connected with the Latin *scindere*, *scidī* 'to cleave' (as in Modern English 'rescind') and they were therefore respelt *scissors* and *scythe*. Johnson rightly preferred *sithe*, but his high authority was here unavailing. *Coud*, past tense of *can*, was written *could* on supposed analogy with *should* and *would*. You may have noticed that Robert Bridges deliberately restored *coud* in *The Testament of Beauty*, but no subsequent writers of repute have ventured to follow his example. Latin-derived *ancor* was blurred with Greek *anchorite* 'one who draws up or back (from the world)' and so was written *anchor*. To their credit the zoologists retain the form *ancoral* when speaking of the anchor-like feet of parasitic crustacea. *Antony*, from the old Roman name *Antonius*, was somehow linked up with the Greek word *anthos* 'flower' which we find in *anthology* and *polyanthus* and so it was often written *Anthony*. Chaucerian *avantage* and *ava(u)nce*, wrongly thought to contain the Latin prefix *ad-*, were changed to *advantage* and *advance*. French *avant* 'before', from Latin *ab* + *ante*, actually lies behind both these words.

Love of Latin caused men to borrow words once more which had already come into English in a modified form by way of French. These resulting word-pairs or *doublets* seldom remain synonymous. In meaning, as in form, they are no longer associated in the mind of the speaker, however fascinating their histories may be to the student of words: *assoil* –

absolve, benison – benediction, blame – blaspheme, chance – cadence, chapter – capital, count – compute, dainty – dignity, fealty – fidelity, frail – fragile, garner – granary, poor – pauper, purvey – provide, ray – radius, reason – ration (ratio), respite – respect, sever – separate, spice – species, strait – strict, sure – secure, treason – tradition.

The Latin words for 'lawful' and 'kingly' were imported three times in the forms *leal – loyal – legal* and *real – royal – regal* from earlier and later Old French and again from Latin direct. *Leal* is still heard in the Scottish and Northern English phrases 'leal and feal' and 'leal and true': heaven is 'the land of the leal'. *Loyal*, which now means 'faithful in allegiance', was still used in the sense of 'legal, legitimate' by Shakespeare: 'Loyall and naturall boy' (*King Lear* II. i. 86). *Real* is now obsolete, but Chaucer described Jason in *The Legend of Good Women* as 'in appearance as royal as a lion' *of his lok as real as a leoun.* Elsewhere he used both *royal* and *regal* (*the justice regal* rendering *regia censura* of Boethius). He could choose whichever form suited him best for rhythm or rhyme or assonance.

Latin and English became more closely blended than ever before and distinctive suffixes like *-ment* and *-ation* were transplanted into native words. A solitary instance may indeed be found in Wyclif's *one-ment* 'the being (at) one (of man with God)' anticipating later *atonement.* In the sixteenth century we first encounter *acknowledgement, amazement, betterment,* and *merriment.* Somewhat later we find recorded *endearment* (1612), *enlightenment* (1669), *bereavement* (1731), *fulfilment* (1775), and *bewilderment* (1820). Native compounds in *-ation* first appeared in the eighteenth century: *flirtation* (1718), *starvation* (1778), and *botheration* (1801).

As early as the fourteenth century *-able* had been treated as a living formative because it was associated with the independent and unrelated adjective *able* (Latin *habilis* 'easy to be held or handled, handy', verbal adjective formed from *habēre* 'to hold, have'; French *habile* 'clever'). Chaucer used *unknowable,*

Wyclif *understandable*, and Shakespeare *answerable*, *unmatchable*, and *laughable*. *Laughable* was later banned by Victorian precisionists on the ground that it was grammatically a malformation for more logical *laugh-at-able*, but they had forgotten their *Merchant of Venice*: 'Though Nestor swear the jest be laughable' (I. i. 56). Johnson characteristically referred to his biographer Boswell as 'a very clubbable man'. Many Latin verbs were modified in a way peculiar to English among the languages of Western Europe, for they were often formed not from the present stem, as in French, Spanish, and Italian, but from the past participle passive. Such expressions as 'a church dedicate (Latin *ecclēsia dēdicāta*) to St Augustine', 'the devil incarnate', and 'frustrate hope' seemed, to an English ear, to postulate corresponding infinitives 'to dedicate', 'to incarnate', and 'to frustrate'. Past participles without *-d* were already familiar in *cast*, *put*, and *set*, as, indeed, they are still, however tempted we may feel to say *broadcasted* instead of *broadcast*! Thus new verbs were formed with infinitives unknown to Latin: not only *dedicate*, *incarnate*, and *frustrate*, but also *accumulate*, *alienate*, *associate*, *create*, *exaggerate*, *hibernate*, *liberate*, *radiate*, *translate*, *ventilate*, and many others. Such verbs have even been formed from Greek – *dehydrate*; from French – *decapitate*, *facilitate*, and *tolerate*; and even from the native adjective *tidy*, which has produced *titivate* after the pattern of *cultivate*.

Some Latin words retained their original meanings in Elizabethan English and we should be ever on the look-out for this possibility in our reading. *Enormous* meant 'out of the norm, abnormal', *extravagant* 'wandering beyond (the path)', and *extraordinary* 'out of the regular course or order'. *Aggravate* meant 'to add weight to, weigh down', and *ponder* literally 'to weigh'. *Premises* were 'things mentioned previously', and *item* 'also' was still an accountant's term introducing all the sections of a bill except the first, which generally opened with *imprimis*. To *transpire* was 'to breathe through or across',

a compound unknown to Latin. It soon acquired the useful
and delicate meaning 'to become known by degrees, to
emerge from secrecy into knowledge' and, more recently, it
has come to be used loosely in the sense 'to happen'.

As a result of the revival of classical learning English writers
had a superabundant wealth of words at their disposal and the
less prudent and critical ones were led to indulge in exuberance and excess, in 'aureate diction' and 'inkhorn terms'.
From aureate diction the poetry of the Scottish Chaucerians,
King James I, Henryson, Dunbar, Douglas and Lindsay, was
seldom free. Chaucer's English admirer Lydgate was capable
of even greater verbal excesses. In the sixteenth century Sir
John Cheke protested against 'inkhorn terms' which were
the inventions of pedants and which were never heard in the
living speech of the market-place. No less severely did Thomas
Wilson, whose *Art of Rhetorique* (1553) came into Shakespeare's hands, reprimand those who 'affect straunge ynke-
horne termes' and who 'seeke so far for outlandish English
that they forget altogether their mothers language. And I dare
sweare this', he added, 'if some of their mothers were alive,
they were not able to tell what they say: and yet these fine
English clerkes will say, they speake in their mother tongue, if
a man should charge them for counterfeiting the King's English. ... The unlearned or foolish phantasticall, that smelles
but of learning (such fellowes as have seen learned men in their
daies) wil so Latin their tongues, that the simple can not but
wonder at their talke, and think surely they speake by some
revelation.' Shakespeare's audiences were surely alive to the
presentation of the pedantic schoolmaster in *Love's Labour's
Lost*, for they had all met Holofernes in real life. Wilson gave
salutary counsel which was echoed by wise judges of style in
the eighteenth and nineteenth centuries who decried 'excessive
Latinity' and who rightly taught that the competent craftsman
was he who preserved a sense of proportion and who kept the
balance between the several main components of the language

and, more particularly, between the Latin and the native elements.

From the pages of *The Oxford English Dictionary* you may, if you will, glean much accurate and entertaining information about the history of the following Latin words, first recorded in English at the dates given: *arbiter* 1502, *genius* 1513, *pollen* 1523, *acumen* 1531, *folio* 1533, *area* 1538, *sternutation* 1545, *circus* 1546, *axis* 1549, *vacuum* 1550, *species* 1551, *terminus* 1555, *decorum* 1568, *ignoramus* 1577, *omen* 1582, *radius* 1597, *stratum*, *virus* 1599, *premium* 1601, *equilibrium* 1608, *specimen* 1610, *series* 1611, *census* 1613, *arena* 1627, *apparatus* 1628, *veto* 1629, *curriculum* 1633, *formula* 1638, *impetus* 1641, *focus* 1644, *complex* 1652, *honorarium* 1658, *pendulum* 1660, *maximum*, *minimum* 1663, *lens*, *status* 1693, *momentum* 1699, *nucleus* 1704, *inertia* 1713, *propaganda* 1718, *auditorium* 1727, *ultimatum* 1731, *insomnia* 1758, *prospectus* 1777, *addendum* 1794, *habitat* 1796, *duplex* 1817, *omnibus* 1829, *animus* 1831, *sanatorium* 1840, *consensus* 1854, *moratorium* 1875, *referendum* 1882, *bacillus* 1883.

This list might be extended considerably. A complete list would include many technical terms which are not in general use. Even in this short list some words appear which seem to have adequate native synonyms. Is *sternutation* different from *sneezing* or *insomnia* different from *sleeplessness*? For the latter French has only *insomnie* and German only *Schlaflosigkeit*, but English is fortunate, I think, in possessing the equivalents of both. There are occasions when it is useful and valuable to have two terms at command with their differing nuances, however slight. Our language gains thereby in precision and power.

Many Englishmen of the sixteenth century wrote their native tongue with the memory of Latin rhythms and cadences in their heads and many others vacillated between the two languages before embarking on work for publication. Roger Ascham remarked casually that it would have been easier for him to write *Toxophilus* in Latin. Sir Thomas More actually did write his *Utopia* in Latin (1516), which was translated into French in his lifetime (1531), but not into English until many years (1551) after his tragic death. Francis Bacon regarded Latin as the one permanent vehicle of learning and he took care to publish his more important treatises in that language. *The Advancement of Learning*, it is true, appeared in English, but *De Augmentis*, its later expanded version, was given to the world (1623) in the language of Cicero. To express oneself in English, averred Edmund Waller the poet, is 'to write in sand'. Even William Harvey, who expounded his discovery of the circulation of the blood to the College of Physicians in the year of Shakespeare's death, thought it best to record the final results of his researches (1628) in Latin.

The notion of uniformity in speech habits was not yet prevalent. Nevertheless, from the fourteenth century onwards,
no other city, with the one possible exception of Edinburgh,
has vied with London seriously. Neither the large and flourish-
ing cities of Bristol and Norwich nor the ancient university
towns of Oxford and Cambridge had ever offered competition
with London in the linguistic field. The other great cities of
England – Birmingham, Liverpool, Manchester, Leeds, Bradford, and Sheffield – are all of later growth.

The diversity of London speech is partly responsible for
those dialectal or abnormal pronunciations of certain words
which, in spite of strong levelling tendencies, have become
generalized in the standard language: words such as *bury*,
ember (in 'ember days'), *left* (as opposed to *right*), *fledge*, *hem-
lock*, *knell*, and *merry*, which still retain their Kentish vowel
sound of short *e* instead of the short *i* of East Midland. The
verb *to bury* and the substantive *burial* show Kentish pronunciation and Southern orthography. The amazingly irregular
sounds of *one* and *once* come from a Southern dialect, for
they have their counterparts in *wuk* and *wuts* for *oak* and *oats*
from Old English *āc* and *āt(an)*. Evidently Old English *ān*
'one' became Southern dialectal *wun*, later [wʌn], by way of
[ɔ:n], [o:n], and [u:n]. Other Southern forms established in
standard speech are *vane* (in 'weather-*vane*'), *vat*, *vent* (slit at
the back of a coat), and *vixen* (female *fox*), which show that
voicing of initial fricative consonant so characteristic of present-day Somerset. The normal East Midland forms would be
fane (as in Chaucer: 'O stormy poeple . . . ever untrewe . . .
and chaungyng as a *fane*'), *fat* (as in Shakespeare and the
Authorized Version), *fent* (as in French *la fente*), and *fixen* (as
in German *die Füchsin*). The sound of the stressed vowel in
among, rhyming with *sung* and not with *song*, comes from the
West Midland dialect, as well as the sound of the stressed
vowels in *monger* and *mongrel*. From the North come *bairn*,
cairn, *hale* (a variant of *whole*), *laird* (from Northern Middle

English *laverd*, corresponding to Southern *lord*), *raid* (a variant of *road* in *inroad*), and *uncouth*.

Sixteenth-century writers were apt to be all too conscious of the disordered state, as they thought it to be, of the English language. Latin, they felt, had its well-tried grammars, its dictionaries, its ancient canons of composition and rules of diction. Latin had models for every occasion and it was thoroughly well taught. The language of Cicero, they rightly felt, was the most teachable subject in the world: English seemed wild and chaotic. Above all, English still lacked a simple all-purpose style.

The man who did more than any other to create a simple all-purpose prose style in the sixteenth century was William Tyndale. Before him there had been various stylistic traditions: the literary prose of Caxton, Malory, and Berners; the expository style of Capgrave, Fortescue, and Pecock; and the emotive prose of the great devotional books of the Middle Ages descending in an unbroken line from *Ancrene Riwle* through Richard Rolle's *Form of Living*, Walter Hilton's *Scale of Perfection*, and the anonymous *Cloud of Unknowing*. Tyndale owed something to all three traditions, but his main strength was his own. His gifts as a writer of simple musical narrative were fully revealed in his translation of the New Testament in 1525. Like all masters of language, he wrote for the ear and not for the eye. When he read aloud his translations to the merchants of Antwerp, the words, we are told by one listener, 'proceeded so fruitfully, sweetly, and gently from him, much like to the writing of John the Evangelist, that it was a heavenly comfort and joy to the audience to hear him read the scriptures'. With Tyndale modern English prose began. One third of the King James Bible of 1611, it has been computed, is worded exactly as Tyndale left it. Such forms as *grece* or *grees* for 'degrees, steps, or stairs', *scrauleth* for 'creepeth', *eareth* for 'plougheth', *raynes* for 'linen' (the linen of Rennes in Brittany), *borde* for 'table', and *herbroulesse* for 'harbourless, as a stranger' were naturally modernized by King James's scholars. So, too, were constructions like *to us ward* and *to his burying ward* showing the old divided preposition. But the revisers were intelligently conservative: they knew their task, and their respect for the majestic simplicity of Tyndale's language was profound.

Tyndale's prose was, indeed, no miracle. He wrote simply because he was in earnest. With the creative artist's certainty of choice, he chose the best of the spoken idioms of his day. He went steadily on and he said plainly and directly just what he meant to say. Was his task, then, easier than that of a twentieth-century writer? It was easier in so far as the English language itself was then more direct and more emphatic. English had at last reached its early maturity. Words were still clean and bright: they had not lost their sharp, cutting edge. Words had not yet gathered about themselves all those connotations, associations and subauditions which, for both good and evil, cling to a language so widely diffused as ours and with such a long literary tradition already behind it. That acute and incisive critic George Saintsbury, who was not given to exaggerate, spoke well when he declared (in his *History of Elizabethan Literature*) that the King James Bible of 1611 is 'probably the greatest prose work in any language. ... The plays of Shakespeare and the English Bible are, and ever will be, the twin monuments not merely of their own period, but of the perfection of English, the complete expressions of the literary capacities of the language, at the time when it had lost none of its pristine vigour, and had put on enough but not too much of the adornments and the limitations of what may be called literary civilization.'

In the next chapter, when considering the more general aspects of sounds and spelling, we shall have occasion to observe the changes made in the qualities of vowel sounds from Chaucer to Shakespeare. In some ways it is easier for us to read Chaucer with the contemporary pronunciation than to read Shakespeare. Chaucer's spelling was more phonetic. If we read, say, the Prologue to the *Canterbury Tales* aloud, trying hard to give each letter its phonetic value and to follow the natural rhythm of the verse, we shall not go so very far wrong. Without some preparation we may slip up on relatively small points, such as the pronunciation of *ou* and *ow* as long *u* [u:], [ou], or [ɔu]. Reliable phonetic transcriptions and gramophone recordings are now available and, having committed the first forty or fifty lines to memory, we may proceed on our own with a fair degree of confidence. The pleasure of reading Chaucer's matchless poetry aloud is its own reward. The accurate reading of Shakespeare's plays is no less rewarding, but it presents more complex problems in some ways. We are more tempted to modernize and the spelling, being less phonetic, does not help us so much. As in the modern Anglo-Irish dialect, *see* and *sea* are not homophones. *Heap* [he:p] does not normally rhyme with *keep* [ki:p] nor *speak* [spe:k] with *seek* [si:k]. The early printers attempted to distinguish between these two sounds, spelling the first with *ea* and the second with *ee* and *ie*, but they were not always consistent. Shakespeare's consonants were pronounced very much as they are to-day, but their precise values have not been fully determined. The *k* was still sounded in *knave* and *knight* and the *g* in *gnat* and *gnaw*. The omission of *l* in *should* and *would* was a vulgarism and even the unetymological *l* in *could* seems to have been pronounced. In careful speech the endings *-sion* and *-tion* were uttered as two syllables: *nation*, for example, as [ne:si-ən] with three syllables as in modern German. The *r* was sounded in various ways, but it was still pronounced in all positions. There was no possibility of confusion between *alms* and *arms* or between *Leah* and *Lear*.

Shakespeare's accentuation often differed from ours. The verbs *'advertise*, *'canonize*, *'demonstrate*, *'envy*, and *perse'vėre* were all stressed on the second syllable thus: *ad'vertise*, *ca'nonize*, *de'monstrate*, *en'vy*, and *per'sever*. Other words with different stresses were *a'spect*, *cha'racter*, *'secure*, and *wel'come*. Sometimes stress was variable: *'commendable* and *com'mendable*, *'confessor* and *con'fessor*. When it preceded a noun *'complete* was stressed thus on the first syllable; in other circumstances it was stressed on the second syllable, as in Modern English.

Already in Elizabethan English the process of shedding inflexional endings had been carried very nearly to its utmost limit with the notable exception of the *-eth* and *-s* endings of the third person singular of the present tense of verbs. In dialects, past and present, people say *he go* for *he goeth* and *he goes*, and there is no reason whatever why this further simplification should not have been accepted by the generality of speakers. The modern *-s* ending came from the north and in Shakespeare's generation it was far commoner in colloquial speech than in literary language. The older *-eth* continued to be regarded as more dignified and permanent. There is no *-s* ending in the First and Second Books of Common Prayer or in the King James Bible. Paradoxically, *doth*, *hath*, and *saith* seem to have been frequently used in conversation, too, and they were the only forms with *-eth* which were contracted to monosyllables. The partial assimilation of *-th* to *-t* after certain consonants, which was still normal in Chaucer's time, as in *arist*, *bit*, and *stant*, for *ariseth*, *biddeth*, and *standeth*, is manifest in Shakespeare only in the verb *list* 'desires, pleases': 'Goe to bed when she list, rise when she list, all is as she will' (*Merry Wives*, II. ii. 124-5). Even this form must have been regarded as old-fashioned, for elsewhere Shakespeare used *listeth* and *lists*.

Because the shedding of inflexional endings was nearly complete the relations between form and function were weakened and no one was more venturesome than Shakespeare himself in making sport of all the old 'parts of speech'. He 'did what he liked with English grammar and drew beauty and power from its imperfections'. He could rely upon his audience to co-operate with him, since these were the days of the nimble wits with their quick linguistic give and take. This kind of word-play, the use of noun as verb and verb as noun, would have been quite impossible in Old English, where the relation between form and function had been close. It was no more possible to use *nama* 'name' as a verb 'to name', instead of *namian*, than it is to use *nōmen* in Latin instead of *nōmināre* or *Name* in German instead of *nennen*. Only with the weakening of inflexions in Middle English and their complete loss in Modern English did this astounding feature of our language, known technically as *conversion*, become feasible. Shakespeare was probably the first to use *window* as a verb in the sense *to place in a window* ('Wouldst thou be window'd in great Rome?': *Antony and Cleopatra*, IV. xii. 72) and *to make full of holes* ('Your looped and window'd raggedness': *King Lear*, III. iv. 30). Shakespeare used adverb as verb ('That from their own misdeeds askance their eyes': *Lucrece*, 637), or as substantive ('In the dark backward and abysm of time': *The Tempest*, I. ii. 50), or as adjective ('Blunting the fine point o? seldom pleasure': *Sonnet*, lii). He used substantive as attribute in 'household words' (*Henry the Fifth*, IV. iii. 52). He spoke of 'far-off mountains' and the 'world-without-end hour'. For the first time, so far as is known, Shakespeare spoke of 'cudgelling one's brain', 'falling to blows', 'breathing one's last', 'beggaring all description', and 'backing a horse'. We now hear such expressions every day and they cease to surprise us because our language has fully adapted itself to such usages. We may now speak of 'making hay *while* (conjunction) the sun shines, thinking it worth our *while* (substantive) thus to *while* (verb) away our time'. It is clear that in this one sentence *while* performs three separate grammatical functions or, in other words, it is used as three different parts of speech. No one who is acquainted only with the living language as it is, or, to use the more fashionable expression, no one who studies this sentence synchronically (and not diachronically or historically), would venture to say which of these three uses is the

original one and which two are 'conversions'. As a matter of
fact, *while* was first a substantive meaning 'time of rest'. In
Old Norse *hvíla* acquired the concrete signification 'bed' and
in Modern Danish *hvile* means 'repose, refreshment'. Those
who are acquainted with the series of consonantal changes
which took place in the passage from Indo-European to Common Germanic, and which go by the name of Grimm's Law
or the First Sound Shifting, will readily associate Old English
hwīl with Latin tran*qu*illus and Modern English tran*qu*il.
We might well suspect that the substantive *down* in North and
South Downs is somehow related to the adverb *down* in spite
of its completely opposite meaning. The history of this word
is most interesting and other factors besides grammatical conversion are involved. *Down* is doubtless of Celtic provenance
(Old Irish *dún* 'hill-fort', Modern Welsh *din*) and it is, in fact,
a distant variant of the *dune* in 'sand-dune', which was adopted
into English from French in the late eighteenth century and
was at first applied specifically to the great sand-hills on the
coast of France and the Netherlands. French had itself taken
the word from Dutch, and Dutch in its turn from Celtic.
Already in late Old English *of dūne* 'from the hill', showing
the dative inflexional *-e*, had become weakened to *adūne* (giving the poetic variant *adown* as, for example, in Scott's
Marmion: 'His gorgeous collar hung *adown*') and then, by
aphesis and apocope (loss of initial and final unstressed syllables), *adūne* became *dūn* and was written *doun* or *down* by
Norman scribes just as *hūs* was written *hous*. 'Doun cam the
reyn' wrote Chaucer in his *Legend of Good Women*, anticipating the very words of a modern popular song. We may now
use *down* as an adjective ('the down platform'), as a preposition ('down the hill'), or as a verb ('to down tools'), and the
wheel of functional adaptation comes full circle when we
speak of 'the ups and downs of life', making *down* a substantive once more. The word *round* has likewise come to perform
varied functions since Shakespeare's day. It may be used as a

substantive ('the daily round of duties'), as an adjective ('the round table'), as an adverb ('The wheel turns round'), as a preposition ('He walked round the estate'), and as a verb ('The ship rounded the Cape of Good Hope'). Which of these five functions is the primary one? No answer can be given without knowledge of the history of this word, which came into English in the thirteenth century from Latin by way of French. Originally *round* was an adjective meaning 'wheel-shaped', Latin *rotundus* 'shaped like a *rota* or wheel'. *Rota*, *rotund*, *rotundity*, and *rotunda* are all, therefore, related words, which were not in general use, however, until after the Restoration. Day by day we may now speak in ordinary conversation of 'letting *bygones* be *bygones*' or of 'ceasing to fret about *might-have-beens*'. We may 'ape our betters' or 'lord it over others'. Misfortune may '*dog* our steps'. The rich and the poor become 'the *have-gots* and the *have-nots*'. If we are energetic and acquisitive we are said to be 'on the *go*' and 'on the *make*': we all like to feel that we are still fully active and well informed, in other words, 'in the *swim*' and 'in the *know*'. Such sayings evince a verbal audacity which is in complete accord with the best Elizabethan traditions. 'No other half-century', Henry Bradley once observed (in his essay on *Shakespeare's English*), 'has done so much for the permanent enrichment of the language as that which is covered by Shakespeare's lifetime.'

When, a generation or so later, the famous Royal Society for the Advancement of Experimental Philosophy was founded in London, its first members were much concerned with language, and in the December of 1664 they went so far as to elect a committee of twenty-two men 'to improve the English tongue particularly for philosophic purposes' and this committee included Dryden, Evelyn, Sprat, and Waller in its number. Dryden excelled in all three fields of creative literature – in prose, poetry, and drama – and he felt all the true artist's restlessness and 'divine discontent'. It was a 'national scandal', he declared, that the English people 'had no prosody' nor 'so much as a tolerable dictionary, or a grammar; so that our language is in a manner barbarous'. He said that he envied the Italians and the French because they had already founded their Academies. Thomas Sprat, Bishop of Rochester, the Society's historiographer, hoped to witness the establishment of an 'impartial Court of Eloquence according to whose censure all books or authors should either stand or fall'. The new scientists, he averred (in his *History of the Royal Society*), should deliberately 'reject all the amplifications, digressions, and swellings of style; returning back to the primitive purity, and shortness, when men delivered so many things, almost in an equal number of words'. They should exact from all the members of the Society 'a close, naked, natural way of speaking; positive expressions; clear senses; a native easiness: bringing all things as near the mathematical plainness as they can; and preferring the language of artisans, countrymen, and merchants, before that of wits or scholars'. Similar recommendations to preachers were made by the Society's first Secretary, John Wilkins, afterwards Bishop of Chester. In *Ecclesiastes or The Gift of Preaching* he proclaimed that the language of the pulpit should be clear, plain, and direct. Such language was certainly effective in his day when he and Edward Stillingfleet, John Tillotson and Robert South, held large congregations as by a spell.

It was in the seventeenth century, and more particularly within the lifetime of Dryden (1631–1700), that the English language may be said to have attained full maturity. All those complex changes and developments, all those adoptions and adaptations which had contributed to the making of English over so many centuries had achieved in the year 1700 a certain balance or equilibrium. It was a very substantial achievement, and if the men of the early eighteenth century were too optimistic and mistook equilibrium for stability, they can scarcely be blamed. Bunyan had already given to the world *Pilgrim's*

Progress (1678), a performance which would have been utterly impossible without the example and inspiration of Tyndale and Coverdale and the Authorized Version. Swift had just finished writing *The Battle of the Books* and *A Tale of a Tub*. Defoe, the future author of *Robinson Crusoe* (1719), was busy with the first of his notorious prose pamphlets.

Bunyan, Swift, and Defoe, in their different ways, showed the powers of a mature and well-balanced English style, a style not far removed from the leisured conversation of the England of their age, but possessing in itself the timeless attributes of all good speech: sincerity, clarity, and vigour. Since the year 1700 the English language has grown in a hundred ways. But its fundamental and structural features, the patterns of its sentences and the forms of its words, have not materially changed.

CHAPTER VI

Sounds and Spelling

FORTY-FOUR sounds are heard in the Queen's English as normally spoken: twelve vowels, nine diphthongs, and twenty-three consonants. Very few languages in the world have so many vowels and diphthongs as this, but unfortunately they are not always so well 'spaced out' or differentiated by English as by Scottish and Irish speakers. You may amuse yourself by saying aloud the following words, which contain the twelve vowel sounds preceded and followed by the voiced plosives *b* and *d*. A precise indication of the quality of the sound is shown within square brackets in accordance with the narrow transcription of the International Phonetic Association, a colon denoting that the sound is long. This length-denoting colon is by no means essential in narrow transcription but I have used it in this chapter for the sake of clarity.

1	2	3	4	5	6
[iː]	[ɪ]	[ɛ]	[æ]	[ɑː]	[ɒ]
bead	*bid*	*bed*	*bad*	*bard*	*bod(γ)*
[biːd]	[bɪd]	[bɛd]	[bæd]	[bɑːd]	[bɒdɪ]

7	8	9	10	11	12
[ɔː]	[ʊ]	[uː]	[ʌ]	[ɜː]	[ə]
board	*bud*	*booed*	*bud*	*bird*	*cupboard*
		('said boo')			
[bɔːd]	[bʊd]	[buːd]	[bʌd]	[bɜːd]	[kʌbəd]
	(Northern)		(Southern)		

TABLE I

In order not to spoil the sequence of *b–d* forms I have been compelled to give disyllabic *body* and *cupboard*. It so happens that there is no word *bod* in the language and vowel-sound No. 12, heard in the unstressed syllable of *cupboard*, never occurs in a stressed position. *Bud*, illustrating vowel-sound No. 8, must here be given its Northern pronunciation and must be made to rhyme with Southern *good* and *hood*. There are, you will observe, five long sounds, Nos. 1, 5, 7, 9, and 11, but not a single one of these corresponds precisely in quality with the short sound. That is why the phonetic symbols are all different. (These simple symbols, by the way, are well worth knowing. It is good, too, to acquire some elementary knowledge of the way in which the speech organs work.) Try prolonging the short vowel in *bid*, for example, without moving tongue or lips and you will realize at once that it is a lower, more open, and more central sound than *bead*. Try prolonging the short sound of *bod* in *body* and you will find that the word sounds more like *bard* than *board*. As for *bed* and *bad*, these have no long counterparts at all in 'received pronunciation'. Many people, in fact, say *bed* and *bad* with a vowel sound half-long before *-d*, especially at the end of a sentence. No two persons pronounce all these twelve sounds in exactly the same way, and one and the same person will vary his sounds according to circumstances, whether reading aloud to himself, conversing quietly with a friend, contending emphatically in debate, or addressing a large public meeting. Clarity of utterance will largely depend upon the 'spacing out' of vowel sounds, and we can all regulate and improve this at will.

The nine English diphthongs (see Table 2) fall naturally into two groups of five and four according to the quality of the second element, whether 'high' [ɪ] or [ʊ] or 'central' [ə].

Since there is no word *bured* in English I have been compelled to give *cured* to illustrate diphthong No. 21. A *di-phthong* is not so much a 'twofold sound' as a whole series of sounds uttered by the speaker as one syllable, that is, with a single breath impulse, and heard by the person addressed as one unit of sonority. It may be defined as a gliding sound produced by the tongue as it moves or glides from one vowel position in the direction of any other. In English that movement of the tongue is either upwards (Nos. 13 to 17) or towards the centre (Nos. 18 to 21). All nine diphthongs are *falling*, that is, the greater stress lies on the first element. English has no *rising* diphthongs like those in *uovo* 'egg' or *uomo* 'man' in Italian. Diphthongs Nos. 13 and 14 are *narrow*: in making them the tongue moves only a short distance. With most speakers No. 13 is the narrowest of all, so narrow, in fact, that a simple vowel sound readily takes its place, [e:] in Scotland and Northumberland, for example, and [ε:] in Lancashire and Yorkshire.

13	14	15	16	17
[eɪ]	[oʊ]	[aɪ]	[aʊ]	[ɔɪ]
bayed	*bode*	*bide*	*bowed*	*buoyed, Boyd*
[beɪd]	[boʊd]	[baɪd]	[baʊd]	[bɔɪd]

18	19	20	21
[ɪə]	[ɛə]	[ɔə]	[ʊə]
beard	*bared, Baird*	*bored*	*cured*
[bɪəd]	[bɛəd]	[bɔəd]	[kjʊəd]

TABLE 2

As you travel over the country you will observe infinite varieties of these five diphthongs from Scottish to Cockney, and you will rightly conclude that the diphthongs are the least stable of our speech sounds and of the sounds of the Germanic languages in general. The Romance and Slavonic languages have relatively few diphthongs and in this respect those tongues have greater stability. Consonants are, in general, the more permanent elements in a language: they are, as it were, the skeleton. Vowels and diphthongs are, so to speak, the flesh and blood. Vowels are less and diphthongs least stable. There were diphthongs in Old English, some inherited with modifications from Common Germanic and others produced by sound changes within the Old English period itself. All these

Old English diphthongs were lost in Middle English, but new ones were then formed as the outcome of combinative changes.

In the East Midland dialect of Middle English there were no fewer than seven long vowels, two more than in present-day English, and in Chaucer's lifetime, as a result of the incipient diphthongization of [iː] and [uː], a general movement or shuffle of all these long vowels began. This remarkable shuffle, now generally known as the *Great Vowel Shift*, modified the entire vowel harmony of our language. It may be represented by the following simple diagram in which the phonetic symbols have precisely the same values as those indicated by *bead*, *bayed*, etc., above.

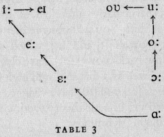

TABLE 3

As the 'high' unstable long vowels [iː] and [uː] became diphthongized, so the next highest long vowels [eː] and [oː] moved up to take their places, leaving room for [ɛː] and [ɔː], and so on. These changes were going on over many generations and in Table 4 they are further illustrated by the history of the sounds in seven simple monosyllables as spoken by Chaucer, Shakespeare, and a present-day speaker, the Roman numerals being the conventional signs for centuries, XIV indicating the fourteenth century, and so on.

(If you have had the patience to read thus far in this book you must be genuinely interested in language and it is clearly worth your while to master, and master accurately, the precise significance of the symbols of the International Phonetic Association which have now won universal acceptance.)

XIV	XIV	XVI–XVII	XX	
Chaucer's spelling	Chaucer's pronunciation	Shakespeare's pronunciation	Present-day pronunciation	Present-day spelling
lyf	liːf	leɪf	laɪf	*life*
deed	deːd	diːd	diːd	*deed*
deel	dɛːl	deːl	diːl	*deal*
name	nɑːmɐ	nɛːm	neɪm	*name*
hoom	hɔːm	hoːm	hoʊm	*home*
mone	moːn	muːn	muːn	*moon*
hous	huːs	hoʊs	haʊs	*house*

TABLE 4

Table 5, which is more detailed, may be skipped without loss if you are not particularly interested in the *chronology* of the Great Vowel Shift. You will observe that the 'high front' and 'high back' vowels [iː] and [uː], which were the first to shift, and the 'low back' vowel [ɑː], have changed more than any other long vowels and that the 'mid high front' and 'mid high back' vowels [eː] and [oː] have changed least. Indeed, if you are interested in phonetic theory, you will soon detect in this table a fascinating symmetry.

XIV	XV	XVI	XVII	XVIII	
iː	ij	eɪ	əɪ	aɪ	*life*
eː	iː				*deed*
ɛː	eː		iː		*deal*
ɑː	æː	ɛː	eː	eɪ	*name*
ɔː		oː		oʊ	*home*
oː	uː				*moon*
uː	uw	oʊ	eʊ	aʊ	*house*

TABLE 5

Most of the sounds indicated by this chronological table may still be heard in living dialects. I have just spent an interesting afternoon listening to the chatter of Scottish children playing in the parks and gardens, the wynds and closes, along and around the Royal Mile from Edinburgh Castle to Holyrood

Palace. In the heart of Midlothian, on the boundary of Old Northumbria, I have discerned many varieties of pronunciation both ancient and modern. Besides normal [nɑʊ] 'now', with the diphthong of 'house' in the above table, I have heard [nuː] as in Old English, [nuw] and [noʊ] as in Tudor times, [neʊ] as in Restoration English, and even [nɑu] with the deep-throated diphthong of Modern German *Haus*.

The four centring diphthongs (Nos. 18 to 21), so characteristic of English, have all arisen from the weakening (in XVII) and the loss (in XVIII) of the rolled or trilled consonant r and the substitution for it of the central and neutral vowel ə. You may practise making this r sound in the various ways known to you, rolling, rattling, trilling, or merely tapping the tongue against the teeth-ridge. In uttering the word *trilling* Londoners form their r by merely curling the tongue-tip backwards after touching the teeth-ridge for *t*, and if, after a vowel, they do not so much as curl the tip but allow the tongue to fall into a neutral position, an ə sound will result. Many pronunciations of *bear* and *bare*, with varieties of r and ə, may be heard to-day. Many speakers who do not normally sound the r of *bear* when it is final in phrase or clause retain it as a *linking* r in expressions like 'I cannot bear it' [aɪ ˈkænɒt ˈbɛər ɪt] and, by analogy, they inadvertently insert it as an *intrusive* r in such locutions as 'the idea of it' [ðɪ aɪˈdɪər əv ɪt].

Just as the loss of final r after a vowel gives rise to a 'centring diphthong', so its loss after any one of the five diphthongs (Nos. 13 to 17) may result in the formation of a 'centring triphthong' (Table 6).

13	14	15	16	17
[eɪ]	[oʊ]	[aɪ]	[aʊ]	[ɔɪ]
payer	sower	buyer	bower	employer
[peɪə]	[soʊə]	[baɪə]	[baʊə]	[ɪmˈplɔɪə]

TABLE 6

These triphthongs may certainly be pronounced as one syllable, but more often in deliberate speech they are heard as two syllables having two 'peaks of prominence' or 'units of sonority'. That is why they are not counted as five separate sounds in our list. Clearly, for example, in reading Shelley's *Ode to a Skylark* we all unconsciously pronounce both *higher* and *fire* as two syllables –

> Higher still and higher
> > From the earth thou springest
> Like a cloud of fire

– for there is no escaping from that lovely rhythm.

Vowels may be defined as voiced sounds made by the breath passing through the mouth in a continuous stream without such narrowing or obstruction as might produce audible friction. Consonants are sounds both voiced or singable, *sonants*, and voiceless or unsingable, *surds*, caused by a partial or complete obstruction of the breath stream. That *narrowing*, *obstruction* or *closure* may be made at eight different points, or by eight different parts of the speech organs, from lips to throat, thus: by the lips, *p*, *b*, *m*, *w*, *wh* [ʍ]; by lips and teeth, *f*, *v*; by the tongue under the front top teeth, voiceless *th* as in 'thin' [θ], voiced *th* as in 'then' [ð]; by the tongue on the teeth-ridge, *t*, *d*, *n*; *l*, *r*; *s*, *z*; by the tongue on gums and hard palate, *sh* [ʃ], *z* as in 'azure' [ʒ]; by the tongue gliding away from the hard palate, *y* as in 'yes' [j]; by the tongue on the soft palate or velum, *k*, *g*, *ng* [ŋ]; and, finally, in the throat or glottis, the tongue lying flat and inactive, *h*. Again, that *narrowing*, *obstruction*, or *closure* may be made in five different ways, thus: by a slight explosion of breath produced by contact and speedy release, the *plosives p*, *b*; *t*, *d*; *k*, *g*; by similar contact and release but with the breath passing through the nose, the nasals *m*, *n*, *ng* [ŋ]; by the front of the tongue touching and spreading over the teeth-ridge and the breath passing through on either side, the *laterals* or varieties of *l*; by the tongue-tip rolling, rattling or tapping against the teeth-ridge, the rolled sounds or varieties of *r*; by the narrowing of the breath-passage so as to cause a rubbing sound, the fricatives f, v; voiceless th as in 'thin' $[\theta]$, voiced th as in 'then' $[\eth]$; s, z, sh $[\int]$, z as in 'azure' $[\mathfrak{z}]$; h; and, finally, by a gliding away of the tongue, the semivowels j, w, the latter having a voiceless counterpart in wh $[\Lambda]$.

These may be regarded as two convenient and practical classifications of the twenty-three consonant sounds of English according to *where* and *how* those sounds are formed. No mention has been made of the *glottal plosive* ['] or of the various *affricatives*, consisting of fricatives following plosives in quick succession and produced by contact and tardy release. Two of these affricatives, however, $[t\int]$ and $[d\mathfrak{z}]$, heard initially and finally in 'church' $[t\int\mathfrak{z}:t\int]$ and 'judge' $[d\mathfrak{z}\Lambda d\mathfrak{z}]$, may well be regarded as 'diphthong consonants' and they may be considered as far too important to leave out of the picture. If we include them, the number of English consonants is raised from twenty-three to twenty-five. If, however, we keep to the lower figure and add to it the twenty-one vowel sounds already enumerated, we arrive at a total of forty-four. Now these forty-four sounds are recorded in writing by means of twenty-six signs or letters. Of these letters three (q, c, and x) are superfluous, inasmuch as they can equally well be represented by k and ks, and one (j), as we have just seen, stands for the compound consonant sound $[d\mathfrak{z}]$. It might be maintained, therefore, that English has only twenty-two effective letters to express exactly twice that number of sounds.

All the alphabets in the world have one common ancestry inasmuch as they all ultimately derive from the *pictograms* of ancient Egypt. Doubtless many men besides the Egyptians devised independent systems of pictograms: the Sumerians, Elamites, Cretans, Hittites, Indians, and Chinese, to name no others. But it so happened that it was from the Egyptian pictograms that those conventionalized pictograms or *ideograms* evolved which, about 1500 B.C., by the process of *phonetization* or the association of sounds with symbols, were modified to form the North Semitic *syllabary*. This particular syllabary, by the principle of *acrophony*, developed into the consonantal *alphabet* of the Phoenicians. Thus, for example, the ideograms for Semitic BETH 'house', GIMEL 'camel', and DALETH 'door' became associated, by acrophony, with the initial sounds uttered in speech, namely, the voiced plosives [b], [g], and [d]. The Greeks learnt this new alphabet from Phoenician seafarers and they adapted it to their own needs by assigning certain unused symbols to the vowel sounds and by adding others. The Romans first became acquainted with Greek writing by way of Etruscan, and their alphabet was in due course transmitted to Britain. The Runic (or national Germanic) alphabet of twenty-four letters was a special adaptation of Greek and Latin for carving on slabs of beechwood, and it was used by the Anglo-Saxons before their conversion to Christianity, when they adopted the Latin alphabet in its British form. In Anglo-Saxon England Germanic runes were still used in inscriptions and Latin letters in manuscripts. After the Norman Conquest French fashions in handwriting, inherited direct from Latin, gradually prevailed and throughout the Middle English period scribes did their best to record sounds clearly and unambiguously. The early printers adhered to these medieval scribal traditions, but long after the invention of movable types, there was no fixed spelling. Indeed, the notion that there is any virtue in uniform spelling is recent. Shakespeare varied the spelling of his own name. Elizabethan compositors varied the forms of words in order to *justify* their lines of type, that is, to make the lines fit in neatly on the page with straight margins. Working with more clumsy types they had less scope than their modern successors, who have much freedom in the arrangement of letters within the line. For mechanical reasons, therefore, the Elizabethans printed *the*, *that*, or γ^e, γ^t; *-lesse*, *-nesse* or *-les*, *-nes*; *manie* or *many*; and so on. Readers were accustomed to see the same word spelt in different ways on one and the same page of a book and, when they came to write themselves, they did very much as they pleased within the borderlines of intelligibility. This is brought home to us when we read the still extant private letters of Sir Ralph Verney of Claydon in Buckinghamshire or of the Reverend Dr Isaac Basire of Durham. Both Verney and Basire were educated men of the seventeenth century, but their spelling now strikes us as whimsical and capricious. Milton himself spelt his pronouns variably, *mee* and *me*, *yee* and *ye*, *shee* and *she*, in order to express degrees of emphasis.

Individuals continued to spell as they pleased, but printers were already exercising economy. In the stress and strain of Civil War the overworked compositor's hand went habitually to the same compartments in his case in setting up particular words and he had little time to devote to the spacing of his lines. Words were weapons of warfare. In publishing polemical pamphlets it seemed frivolous to bother about alternative spellings. Many printers accepted the forms in the first, second and third Authorized Versions of the Bible of 1611, 1629 and 1638 as their models. On the whole, they were well advised to do so. Nevertheless many present-day anomalies. like *aisle*, *blood*, *bread*, *wound*; *have*, *live*, *prove*; *done*, *one*, *none*; *do*, *two*, *who*; *come*, *some*; *any* and *many* can be traced back to the first half of the seventeenth century. These forms eventually found their way into the great eighteenth-century lexicons, Nathaniel Bailey's *Universal Etymological English Dictionary* of 1721 and Samuel Johnson's *Dictionary of the English Language* of 1755. Dr Johnson, the first really authoritative lexicographer, was not interested in the improvement of English orthography. The men, on the other hand, who revised the French Academy Dictionary, published only seven years later (1762), changed the forms of some five thousand words or one quarter of the whole French vocabulary. Johnson did his best to abolish inconsistencies, but his attitude towards traditional spellings was one of conservatism and piety. 'I have attempted few alterations', he said, 'and among these few perhaps the greater

part is from the modern to the ancient practice; and I hope I
may be allowed to recommend to those whose thoughts have
been, perhaps, employed too anxiously in verbal singularities,
not to disturb, upon narrower views, or for minute propriety,
the orthography of their fathers.' The great one-man Dictionary was not, in fact, entirely free from inconsistencies: *moveable* but *immovable*, *downhil* but *uphill*, *distil* but *instill*, *install*
but *reinstal*, *sliness* but *slyly*, *conceit* and *deceit* but *receipt*, *deign*
but *disdain*, *anterior* and *interiour* but *exterior* and *posterior*.
Some of these Johnsonian inconsistencies remain as possible
alternatives to this day, although, for various reasons, the one
or the other form is to be preferred. *Movable* is more acceptable than *moveable*; *distil*, *instil*, and *install* are preferable to
distill, *instill*, and *instal*; and *slyly* and *slyness* are better than
slily and *sliness*. The Elizabethans had displayed irrelevant
learning by restoring the *p* in *conceipt*, *deceipt*, and *receipt*. Johnson's unfortunate inconsistency in respect of these three words
has now become permanent. So, too, have the discrepancies in
deign and *disdain*, deriving from the same root of Latin *dignus*
'worthy' and coming into English from Old French, where
the variants *daign*, *deign*, and *dain* were widespread. As for the
fluctuations between Latin *-or* and Anglo-Norman *-our*, these
anticipate later divergencies between American and British
English. It is interesting to note that Johnson made no distinction in spelling between *flour* and *flower*, although Cruden had
already recognized the modern distinction in his *Concordance*
of 1738. Johnson gave 'the finest part of meal' as one of the
senses of *flower*. Unlike many other authors of the eighteenth
and early nineteenth centuries, he did discriminate between
metal 'a firm, heavy, and hard substance, opake, fusible by
fire' and *mettle* 'spirit, spriteliness, courage', although, it must
be added, these two words are historically one, deriving ultimately from Greek *métallon* 'mine'. In general, Johnson's spellings have been maintained in spite of anomalies. We all read
by syllables rather than by letters. We form pictures of words

by which we apprehend the meaning direct. As Henry Bradley pointed out in his masterly paper *On the Relations between Spoken and Written Language with special reference to English*, first addressed to the International Historical Congress of 1913, it is far more important to the ordinary person that a written word should quickly and surely suggest its meaning than that it should accurately express its sound. 'Speech and writing are two organs for the expression of meaning, originally co-ordinate and mutually independent.'

English spelling is even more unphonetic than French and yet it has manifest advantages. First, the consonants are fairly unambiguous: in general they do faithfully record the sounds. Secondly, by great good fortune English spelling has escaped those tiresome diacritical marks placed above, beneath, before or after the letter, or inserted within it, which in a greater or less degree disfigure French, German, Italian, Spanish, Czech (solely the work of Jan Hus), Polish, Norwegian, Danish, Swedish, and even modern Turkish (unadvisedly introduced by Kemal Ataturk). Thirdly, English spelling conserves the rich and far-reaching international characteristics of our speech so that men of many nations are immediately aware of the meanings of thousands of words which would be unrecognizable if written phonetically. It is, indeed, the striking incompatibility between the native and the Latin elements of our language which presents the greatest obstacle to those drastic reformers who would adopt the principle of one symbol for one sound as their basis. As Sir William Craigie so clearly demonstrated in his S.P.E. Tract of 1944 on *Problems of Spelling Reform*, this is the crux. If the native spelling is retained, much of the Latin and French element becomes unrecognizable. If we take *seed* as the norm, then *cede* and *recede* must become *seed* and *reseed*. If we take *mesh* as the norm, then both *cession* and *session* must become *seshon*, and *fissure* must become identical with *fisher*. If, on the contrary, *fuse* and *muse* are kept, then *news* will be *nuse* and both *hues* and *hews* (in 'he hews') will be *huse*. Again, if *c* were retained before the back vowel in *capital*, *colony*, and *custom*, then some such forms as *senter*, *sertin*, and *sirkel* would have to take the place of *centre*, *certain*, and *circle*. Would a foreign student like to find whole sections of his English vocabulary torn away from their counterparts in those European languages with one or other of which he is probably acquainted? Should *nation* and *national* be written *neishon* and *nashonal* and thus be dissociated from one another in English and from their identical, or nearly identical, forms, not only in the Romance languages like French, Spanish, Portuguese, and Italian, but also in the Scandinavian languages, as well as German and Dutch? Would an English child find self-expression easier if he were taught to write *cats* but *dogz* and *horsez*; *jumps* but *runz* and *rizez*; and *jumpt* but *turnd* and *landed*? Many authors in the seventeenth century, including Milton and Dryden, wrote *mist* for *missed*, and this simple phonetic spelling surely had everything in its favour. In practice, however, it was found to lead to ambiguity and misunderstanding and by general consent it was discarded. As for that butt of so much scorn and obloquy, that notorious *-ough-*group, no satisfactory spellings have ever been devised for all the seven pronunciations represented by *plough*, *trough*, *rough*, *thought*, *through*, *though*, and *thorough*. American *plow* is old and good, but are *bough* and *slough* to be written *bow* and *slow*? American *thru* is brief but unparalleled, and *thruout* is unacceptable. We may all use *tho'* in private correspondence, but we know very well that the apostrophe is irregular and the apostrophe is the nearest approach in English to a diacritical mark, to be avoided, if possible, at all costs. Even the deletion of final *-e*, when it does not fulfil the historical function of denoting a long vowel or diphthong as in *ravine* and *stone*, cannot be applied universally. For example, it must be retained in *hearse*. It might, perhaps, be dropped in words like *infinite* and *doctrine*, even as it has already been discarded in *deposit* and *fossil* and, quite recently, in *proletariat* and *secretariat*. Words like *horrour* and *terrour*, *musick* and *physick*, *chymical* and *chymist* have been changed to *horror* and *terror*, *music* and *physic*, *chemical* and *chemist* within living memory. Gradually these new spellings have 'caught on' and they are now firmly established. We now see *fantasy* superseding *phantasy*. Why not? It is, with a different penumbra of meaning, a variant of *fancy*. We should welcome attempts at improvement and we should encourage editors to be enterprising. Many more words might have two accepted 'correct' spellings side by side. We may follow the Oxford manner and write *abridgement*, *acknowledgement*, and *judgement* on the ground that these forms are more in accordance with English values of letters, but we should not object in the least to the Cambridge fashion of writing *abridgment*, *acknowledgment*, and *judgment*. Let us make up our minds finally about *embarrass* and *harass*, *connexion* and *inclose*, but, having decided arbitrarily to write *biased* and *focusing* ourselves, let us allow others to write *biassed* and *focussing* if they so prefer. It is unreasonable for us to take exception to *program*, *fulfillment*, *dialog*, *center*, and *traveling*, when we encounter these forms in American books and films, even though we ourselves, like Dr Johnson, choose 'not to disturb the orthography of our fathers'. As a matter of fact, the pendulum of fashion across the Atlantic is swinging back towards European English again. Hundreds of discriminatory spellings introduced by Noah Webster into his *Compendious Dictionary of the English Language* of 1828 have been rejected by subsequent editors of that famous lexicon. Many Americans deliberately prefer English forms and the new Merriam-Webster *Pocket Dictionary*, which is now in use all over the world, includes a remarkably high percentage of permissible variant spellings. Many people, however, will be surprised, upon consulting this popular manual, to find no alternative forms in *ise*, for such verbs as *apologize*, *realize*, and *jeopardize*. Now these three verbs all show the Greek suffix *-ízein*, which became *-izāre* in Latin and *-iser* in French. *Apologize*, indeed, shows this verbal suffix added to a Greek word, *realize* to a Latin word, and *jeopardize* to the Anglicized form of a French word. There is much to be said in favour of spelling *apologize*, *realize*, and *jeopardize* in this way as well as *Anglicize* (which I happened to use in the previous sentence), *baptize* (probably the earliest *-ize* verb in English), *characterize*, *economize*, *idolize*, *organize*, *sympathize*; *authorize*, *civilize*, *colonize*, *fertilize*, *nationalize*, and *scrutinize*; *galvanize*, *macadamize*, and *mesmerize*; and many others. You will observe that all these words are thus printed by the Oxford University Press (for example, in the volumes of *The Oxford History of England*), by the Cambridge University Press (for example, in the volumes of *The Cambridge History of English Literature*), by *The Times* newspaper, and by the Americans and Canadians in general. Nevertheless, there are a few fairly common verbs like *apprise*, *comprise*, *enterprise*, *surprise*; *devise*, *improvise*, *supervise*; *despise*, *disguise*, and *surmise*, which do not show Greek-derived *-ize* and which should be spelt *-ise* in spite of identical pronunciation. Is it surprising, then, that many publishing firms ignore the *-ize*/*-ise* distinction altogether and use *-ise* alike for all these verbs? It may be easy enough to separate the compounds *ap-prise*, *com-prise*, *enter-prise*, and so on, into their component parts and thus to demonstrate that no *-ize* suffix is involved, but busy men of affairs do not wish to spend time on such niceties.

In the meantime, 'spelling pronunciations' become more frequent day by day. During the last two centuries, and especially since the passing of the Education Act of 1870, the influence of spelling upon sounds has been constant and considerable. Pope rhymed *join* with *line*, but it was a foregone conclusion that that historical pronunciation of *join* would not hold out for very long against the pull of the spelling. How many people to-day discriminate between *salve* 'to soothe' (as in 'to salve one's conscience'), rhyming with *halve*, and *salve* 'to save (a ship or cargo) from loss', rhyming with *valve*?

Most people still make *clerk* rhyme with *dark*, but they say *merchant service* for the *marchant sarvice* of the nineteenth century. *Rome* now rhymes with *home* and not with the *doom* or *dome* of Domesday Book. This is partly a spelling pronunciation and partly a new pronunciation based upon Italian *Roma*. Chaucer rhymed *Rome* with *to me* and Shakespeare punned on *Rome* and *room*. Such recent 'occasional spellings' as *creater*, *mater*, *obleege*, and *sojer* remind us how pronunciation has since moved in the direction of orthography. Many people now pronounce the *t* in *often* who would not think of doing so in *soften*. The post-dental plosive was regularly lost in this position in the sixteenth century. Queen Elizabeth wrote *offen*. Undoubtedly the pronunciation with *t* will prevail. As a boy I pronounced *often* and *orphan* alike, I now say 'often' with a shortened vowel, and I may decide one day soon to put in the *t*. A man may and should revise his speech-habits from time to time in order to keep pace with life and custom. It is unfortunate that so many of the new pronunciations sound thinner and less sonorous than the old. Of all the influences affecting present-day English that of spelling upon sounds is probably the hardest to resist.

CHAPTER VII

Word Creation

AT all periods in the history of a language a new word may suddenly appear as if from nowhere, or a new word may be deliberately created by one man who tells the world exactly what he is doing. Echoic words like *bang, pop,* and *whizz* or nonsense-syllables like *ta-ra-ra-boom-de-ay* and *a-heigh-and-a-ho-and-a-heigh-nonny-no* form yet a third class, and they are easily accounted for.

Let us take *dog* and *pig* as examples of the first class. The old word for 'dog' is *hound*. So far as is known, *dog* is first recorded in its genitive plural form *docgena*, glossing Latin *canum*, in a twelfth-century manuscript. Its previous origin and history are quite unknown. Not many years later *pig* makes its first appearance in the *Ancrene Riwle*. The old word was *swine*. Other common words of unknown provenance are *bad, big, cut, fog, lad,* and *lass,* which were first employed in the thirteenth and fourteenth centuries; *bet, crease, dodge, gloat,* and *jump* in the sixteenth; *blight, chum, fun, hump,* and *job* in the seventeenth; *bore* (in the sense 'ennui'), *donkey* (first pronounced 'dunkey'; perhaps a pet form of Duncan), *fun, hoax,* and *jam* in the eighteenth. In the nineteenth century we first encounter *slum* and *loaf* in the sense 'to spend time idly'. According to *The Oxford Dictionary* the last word was first used in *Charcoal Sketches* (1838) by Joseph Neal, who evidently regarded it as colloquial or slang because he placed it within inverted commas – 'One night, Mr Dabbs came home from his 'loafing' place – for he 'loafs' of an evening like the generality of people – that being the most popular and the cheapest amusement extant'. A few years later it was used by Dickens in *Martin Chuzzlewit* and by Mrs Beecher Stowe in *Uncle Tom's Cabin*. No one knows its origin. Lowell conjectured that it might come from *lofen*, a dialectal variant of German *laufen* 'to run', which, as we saw in Chapter I, is related to our *leap*. This is a mere guess and yet, though the difference in meaning is so strongly against it, it has been adopted as a plausible etymology by many English and American dictionaries. *The Oxford Dictionary* is more guarded. It mentions Lowell's surmise, but it marks the word as 'of obscure origin'. Under *loafer* 'one who spends his time in idleness' the possibility is mooted that this substantive may be the source of the verb by 'back-formation'. That is all. In nineteenth-century American may be found for the first time *blizzard* (from the storm of 1880), *bogus*, and *rowdy*.

Among the many notable word-creations in the second class let us consider just four: *gas*, *paraffin*, *vaseline*, and *blurb*. These certainly have strange appearances, but no lexicographer, however cautious, need add *etym. dub.* 'etymology dubious' or *of obscure origin* to his account of them, since precise facts are known. In his *Ortus Medicinae* or *Rise of Medicine* (1652) the Dutch chemist J. B. Van Helmont states that he invented the form *gas* on the basis of the Greek *chaos*, the *ch-* or χ- of Greek and the *g-* of Dutch both alike being pronounced as a fricative similar to the *-ch* in Scottish *loch*. As for *paraffin*, this artificial mixture of hydrocarbons was first discovered by the German physicist Karl von Reichenbach in 1830 and he was very much impressed at the time by the remarkably *small affinity* (Latin *parum* 'little' – *affinis* 'having relationship, partaking, sharing') that it possessed with other bodies. Von Reichenbach took these two Latin words, cut off their terminations, and joined them together! It was as simple as that! Some forty years or so later (1872) Robert A. Chesebrough concocted the trade and proprietary name *vas – el – ine* for soft petroleum jelly by adding the suffix *-ine* to the initial syllables of German *Wasser* (*w* – pronounced *v*-) and Greek *élaion* 'oil'. In 1907 the American journalist Gelett Burgess hit upon the bright idea of calling the publisher's 'puff' or eulogy, printed on a book-jacket, the *blurb*. A long and detailed account of the frivolous occasion may be found in the First Supplement (1945) to H. L. Mencken's work on *The American Language*.

Even ancient words may have been compounded on specific occasions, the details of which are known. The Greek thinker Pythagoras resented being called *sophistés* 'wise man, wizard' and so he persuaded his friends to name him *philósophos* 'lover of wisdom' instead. We now use both words in slightly modified forms, *sophist* and *philosopher*. Cicero formed *qualitas* and *indolentia* to render Aristotle's *poiótēs* and *apátheia*, and these have become *quality* and *indolence* in English. *Apathy* means, in the first place, 'insensibility to suffering', but it may still be said to imply 'indolence of mind'.

Chaucer not only imported hundreds of words into English: he also created hundreds. So, too, did the Elizabethan poets, Shakespeare above all. In his *Pseudodoxia Epidemica* or *Vulgar Errors* Sir Thomas Browne introduced ponderous words like *antediluvian*, *hallucination*, *incontrovertible*, *insecurity*, *precarious*, and *retrogression*. Sir Isaac Newton was the first to use *centrifugal* and *centripetal*. Indeed, many words may be traced to individual writers in Newton's century: *central*, *circuitous*, *decorous*, *fortuitous*, and *freakish* to the Cambridge Platonist Henry More; *attitude*, *balustrade*, *cascade*, *contour*, *monochrome*, *opera*, *outline*, and *pastel* to the diarist John Evelyn; and *corpuscle*, *intensity*, *pathological*, and *pendulum* to the natural philosopher and chemist Robert Boyle. Edmund Burke was responsible for *colonial*, *colonization*, *diplomacy*, *electioneering*, *expenditure*, *federalism*, *financial*, and *municipality*. Coleridge introduced *intensify*, *pessimism*, and *phenomenal*; and, in *Biographia Literaria*, he first referred to the period of Queen Elizabeth as 'our golden *Elizabethian* age', Carlyle modifying the epithet to *Elizabethan* in *Heroes and Hero-Worship*. Jeremy Bentham was the first, in the phrase 'the good of the community', to apply the term *community* to the people of a country as a whole. He it was who first used the adjectives *detachable, dynamic, exhaustive, unilateral,* and *international,* the last with a sincere apology! The term *international,* he pointed out in his *Principles of Morals and Legislation* (1780), is 'a new one; though, it is hoped, sufficiently analogous and intelligible. It is calculated to express, in a more significant way, the branch of law which goes commonly under the name of the *law of nations'*. William Whewell likewise apologized for indulging in such unheard-of word-formations as *physicist* and *scientist* in his *Philosophy of the Inductive Sciences* (1840). 'The terminations *-ize, -ism,* and *-ist'*, he claimed, 'are applied to words of all origins: thus we have to *pulverize,* to *colonize; witticism, heathenism; journalist, tobacconist.* Hence we may make such words when they are wanted. As we cannot use *physician* for a cultivator of *physics,* I have called him a *physicist.* We need very much a name to describe a cultivator of science in general. I should incline to call him a *scientist.'* George Eliot was once asked, 'Are you an optimist or a pessimist?' 'Neither,' came the reply, 'I am a *meliorist.'* Macaulay apologized for using *constituency,* but his contemporary Carlyle, that intrepid word-coiner, saw no need to express regret for his word-creations, however eccentric or exotic they might be. Some of his combinations, like *mischief-joy,* translating *Schadenfreude,* are intelligible only to those of his readers who know German. Like Scott, however, he brought such Scottish words into English as *feckless, lilt* (with the meaning of 'cadence'), and *outcome,* and made them current. The now common words *decadent, environment,* and *self-help* seem to have been Carlyle's own. Shaw translated Nietzsche's *Übermensch* as *superman* – others had previously rendered it *beyondman* and *overman* – and set the fashion in *super* words, especially in America, where linguistic exuberance has produced *super-colossal*, *super-maximum*, *super-ultra*, *super-superlative*, and even *super-super*.

If we compare Shaw's *superman* with such a common component as *workman* we are at once conscious of a difference. *Workman* is made up of two nouns juxtaposed, the precise relationship between them being not easy to define. *Workman* first appears in a very famous passage in King Alfred's version of Boethius in which he formulates that tripartite division of medieval society into *gebedmen 7 fyrdmen 7 weorcmen* 'the men who pray, the men who fight, and the men who work'. English has many thousands of such compounds, formed at various periods, their component parts showing diverse relationships of which the speaker may or may not be conscious. Why do we say *townsman* but *countryman*? Consider the relationship between *boat* and *house* in *house-boat*, 'boat fitted up like a house for living in', and *boat-house*, 'house or shed at the water's edge in which boats are stored'. Compare the functions of *sun* in *sunrise* and *sunset*, denoting the subject of the action; in *sun-worship*, denoting the object; in *sunspot*, denoting the place; in *sundial*, denoting the co-operating agent; in *sunbeam* and *sunlight*, denoting the source; in *sunflower*, denoting that it is the object followed (Latin *solsequium*, Middle English *solsecle*) or turned to (Greek *heliotrope*, Tudor English *turnsole*), or the object of resemblance. Contrast the divergent functions of the first elements in *schoolboy* 'boy going to school', *bedroom* 'room furnished with a bed or beds', *wheelwright* 'maker of wheels', *windmill* 'mill driven by the wind', *rainbow* 'bow formed by the sun on falling rain', *flagstaff* 'pole on which a flag is displayed', *road-sense* 'sense of direction and capacity for the handling of a vehicle on the road', *airman* 'man who navigates an aircraft through the air', *airlift* 'transport by freight planes', *airway* 'route regularly followed by aircraft'. Such compounds are valuable in speech because they are so much more concise and economical than the corresponding circumlocutions. There is surprisingly little ambiguity because, after a time, the precise signification is fixed by usage. English has illogically extended the *grand* of *grand-father* to *grandson* 'one's child's son'. French *grand* in *grand-père* means 'of great age': *grandson* in French is *petit-fils* 'little son' and *grand-fils* would surely sound ridiculous. But the use of *grandson* leads to no misunderstanding since it is shown to be a compound by stress and tone. Without thinking about it, we naturally speak of a *good-tempered* dog (a dog with a good temper) but of *well-tempered* steel (steel tempered well). The statement that 'a blackbird is a black bird' is true of the male only, for the female is brown. A child will quite naturally point to 'a brown blackbird' on the lawn.

The wealth and resourcefulness of English in the formation of derivatives may be illustrated by a study of all the words springing from the native root *bear* and the Latin *ced*. Some forty other words, ranging from *birth* to *overburdensome*, have been formed from *bear* during the course of ten centuries. The Latin root *ced* 'go from', with its participial form *cess-* and its related French form *cease*, has been yet more prolific and has produced no fewer than eighty derivatives. Many of these have been formed by means of classical and native affixes which, for the most part, still live and thrive.

Let us consider, for example, the various prefixes that may still be used to express negation. There is, first of all, the Greek *a-*, or 'privative alpha', as in *amorphous*, *apathetic*, and *atheist*; becoming *an-* before vowels as in *anaemia*, *anaesthesia*, *anarchy*, *anodyne*, and *anonymous*. Then there is the Latin *in-* as in *in-accessible*, *inaudible*, *incorrect*, *incredible*, *intangible*, and *invisible*; becoming *il-*, *im-*, and *ir-* before certain consonants as in *il-legal*, *illegible*, and *illicit*; *immature*, *immediate* 'not separated by any intervening medium', and *immortal*; *irrational*, *irremedi-able*, and *irresponsible*. Further, Latin and French *non-* is used in *nonchalance* and *nonpareil*, as well as *noncombatant*, *nonconductor*, *nondescript*, and *nonjuring*. Germanic *un-*, as in *ungodly*, *unjust*, *unkind*, *unknowable*, and *unutterable*, is probably the commonest negative prefix of all, but it should be dissociated from the other *un-* prefix of quite different origin which denotes reversal or deprivation as in *unbind*, *unbutton*, *uncover*, *undo*, *unlock*, and *unpack*. Old English *ne-*, becoming *n-* before vowels, is manifest in *neither*, *never*, *none*, and *nor*; whereas Modern English *no-* appears in *no-ball*, *no-confidence*, and *no-thoroughfare*. Having such an abundance of prefixes to choose from, people sometimes vacillate between two forms. It is, after all, usage alone that determines us in saying *inexpressible* but *unexpressive*, *impracticable* but *unpractical*, *irresponsible* but *unresponsive*. Northern children still say *unpossible* and they are liable to be rebuked by their elders for using an expression that is 'vulgar' or 'substandard'. This was, in fact, the commoner form from Langland to Dryden and it was the only form in the King James Bible, having been silently changed to *impossible* in later editions of the Authorized Version. It is interesting to observe that in current philosophical writings we find three living prefixes still competing for recognition in the terms *amoral*, *unmoral*, and *nonmoral*. To the student of ethics or moral science these adjectives all mean the same thing, namely 'beyond the sphere of morals, unconcerned with morality', as distinct from the more general term *immoral* 'opposed to morality, morally evil, vicious'.

Two prefixes now enjoying an extraordinary vogue are the Greek *anti-* 'against' and the Latin *extra-* 'outside'. In a healthy democracy vigilance implies opposition. 'The political history of the United States', it has been said, 'might be written in terms of those opposition movements which employed this derivational element, ranging all the way from *anti-Federalist* and *anti-Republican* to *anti-New-deal* and *anti-Marshall-aid*'. Opposition was only one of the meanings of *anti* in Greek. It may now denote a counter-movement as in *anti-feminism*, *anti-squandermania*, and *anti-vivisectionism*; or it may be prefixed to a substantive with prepositional force as in *anti-aircraft* (battery), *anti-tank* (gun), and *anti-trade* (wind). From the phrase *extrā ordinem* 'outside the regular order' the Romans constructed the adjective *extrāordinārius*, but otherwise *extrā* did not figure as a prefix in classical Latin. In seventeenth-century English *extraparochial*, *extraprovincial*, and *extraterritorial* were first used as legal and administrative terms and in more recent times numerous adjectives of this type have been formed. *Extraordinary*, shortened to *extra*, may now be attached to any epithet and may itself be used as adjective ('extra pay for extra work'), adverb ('to work extra hard') and substantive ('wine is an extra'), not only in English but also in French and German and, in the form *estra*, in Spanish and Italian also.

Another prefix which has been resuscitated in recent years is the Latin *semi-*. We now speak of *semi-darkness*, *semi-open-air*, *semi-wild*, and *semi-occasionally*. *Semi-annual* is sometimes preferred to *half-yearly* and *semi-centennial* is used in the sense 'occurring every fifty years'. Even Old English had the two prefixes *healf-* and *sam-*, the latter still surviving in dialectal *sam-hale* 'half-whole, in poor health' and *sam-sodden* 'half cooked, half done', applied derisively to persons, just as in modern slang people say 'half baked' for 'stupid'. Even these prefixes are not always interchangeable. In order to be understood we must say 'half-time in the semi-final (football match)' and not 'semi-time in the half-final'. Besides *semi-* and *half-* we have *hemi-* from Greek and *demi-* from French, the latter going back to Latin *dīmidium* from *dis + medius* 'divided into two equal parts from the middle'. Chaucer used *hemisphere* to denote one half of the celestial globe as seen above the horizon and the Elizabethans called a half-line of verse a *hemistich*. *Demi-* was first employed in heraldry in the fifteenth century to indicate the half-length figure of a man or animal, or half of a charge or bearing, as in *demi-angel* and *demi-vol* 'a single wing of a bird'; in the sixteenth century it came to be used in names of guns and armour as in *demi-cannon* and *demi-cuirass*, and it was soon extended to other

uses. Musicians, who inherit their nomenclature from the days
of plain chant, speak of *demicrotchets* or quavers and they have
recourse to all three classical prefixes meaning 'half' when
they call a note a *hemidemisemiquaver* if it is equal to a
sixty-fourth part of a semi-breve, or a *quasihemidemisemiquaver*
if it is equal to a one hundred and twenty-eighth part.

The hyphen, which was unknown in Old and Middle English, is still used somewhat loosely. Its function should be that
of marking the progress or transition of a new compound
from two words to one, as, for example, from *book mark* to
book-mark to *bookmark*, or from *no body* (xiv–xviii) to *nobody* (xvii–xviii) to *nobody* (xix–xx). Such transitions in-
volve changes in intonations and stress. Yet we still write
highway but *High Street*. The hyphen is often employed to
avoid obscurity or to mark a distinction. To *recount* means 'to
narrate', but to *re-count* means 'to count again'. We *reform* our
way of life but we *re-form* our broken ranks; we *recollect* the
past, but we *re-collect* things that have been distributed. Sometimes it is essential thus to differentiate between words of
diverse origin and meaning: to *re-coil* a rope (French *cueillir*),
but to *recoil* from danger (French *se reculer*); to *re-cover* an old
umbrella (Latin *cooperīre*), but to *recover* a lost umbrella (Latin
recuperāre); to *re-lay* a cable or a flagstone path (English *lay*,
factitive form of *lie*), but to *relay* a message (Old French *relais*
'a set of fresh hunting-dogs or horses'); to *re-pair* animals for
breeding (Latin *par* 'equal'), but to *repair* to the next village
(Late Latin *patriāre* from *patria* 'native land', as in English
repatriate) and to *repair* a broken fence (Latin *parāre* 'to make
ready').

In a previous chapter we have seen how the medical specialists endowed the old Greek suffixes *-itis* and *-osis* with new
semantic content, and if we keep our eyes open in this quickly
changing world, we shall discover other similar manifestations
in the language around us. Beginning with the phoneme,
philologists pass on to speak about *morphemes*, *taxemes* or

tagmemes, sememes (including *pleremes* and *kenemes*), *tonemes,* and *chronemes,* as if *-eme* were a brand-new suffix meaning 'linguistic agent'. Meantime the literary critics have bestowed a new signification upon the ancient colourless suffix *-ese* of *Chinese* and *Japanese* meaning 'belonging to a place', related to Latin *-ēnsis* in *Athēniēnsis* 'Athenian' and *Eborācēnsis* 'pertaining to the city of York' and seen in French *anglais,* Italian *inglese,* and Spanish *inglés.* As long ago as 1843 Macaulay described a ponderous Latinized style as *Johnsonese.* Matthew Arnold advised a young friend who was anxious to acquire a sound and sensible prose style to 'flee *Carlylese* as the very devil'. 'Newspaper or penny-a-liner's English' was dubbed *journalese* in 1882 and, since then, various undesirable types of English have been labelled *newspaperese* (1889), *guidebookese* (1906), and *officialese* (1927).

In language as in life it is not easy to assess the power and determine the direction of movements and trends in the world around us, but the interested observer can hardly fail to perceive certain indications that the tide of analytic tendencies in English is on the turn and that the latent synthetic qualities of our heterogeneous language are once more asserting themselves. The rhythmic transitions from synthesis to analysis and from analysis to synthesis are the systole and the diastole of the human heart in language. The old inflexions of Indo-European are gone for ever. Gothic *weis habaidedum* is English *we had.* 'English', as Sapir acutely remarked, 'is only analytic in tendency. Relatively to French, it is still fairly synthetic, at least in certain respects.' In the resuscitation of old affixes and in the creation of new ones English is showing these synthetic powers. Without growth and change there is neither life nor vigour in language. When the leader-writer devised the clever headline SCHOLARSHIPS NOT BATTLESHIPS, he knew very well what he was doing! The Old English *-ship,* related to *shape* and to *scape* in *landscape* (Dutch *landschap*), is very much alive. Witness *marksmanship, dictatorship,* and *airmanship.* Because the suffix -*ship* is fully alive it can be constructed with words of many origins: *directorship* and *dictatorship*, Latin + English; *courtship*, French + English; *trusteeship*, Scandinavian + French + English. Hybrids luxuriate in the English word-garden. We do not feel unkindly towards *scarceness* because it is compounded of Latin + English; *priesthood*, Greek +English; *talkative*, English + Latin; *musical*, Greek + Latin; *beautiful*, French + English; *lovable*, English + French; *huntress*, English + Greek; *bureaucracy*, French + Greek; *colonize*, Latin + Greek; and *macadamization*, Celtic + Hebrew + Greek + Latin. We refer, too often ambiguously, to the *pre-war*, the *post-war*, and even the *inter-war* years. We speak of the *pros* and *cons*, things for and against, when we really mean *pros* and *contras*. We share with French our most elaborate derivative *in-com-pre-hen-s-ib-il-it-y*, with its root *hen* and its eight affixes and infixes. *Unbegreiflichkeit*, its German equivalent, is weighty enough, but its structure is simpler.

Apart from inherited formative elements new words are daily created in scores of other ways. The pleasing antiphony of *ding-dong*, *ping-pong*, and *sing-song* is varied in *dingle-dangle*, *dilly-dally*, *fibble-fabble* (from *fibble-fable*, a playful elaboration of *fable*, whence our *fib*), *flim-flam*, *flip-flop*, *riff-raff*, Shakespeare's *skimble-skamble*, *shilly-shally* (probably from the old subjunctive *shill I* alternating with the old indicative *shall I*), *tittle-tattle*, and *zig-zag*. The playful iterations with change of initial consonant in *hoity-toity* and *namby-pamby* (from Ambrose Philips) are extended to *hanky-panky* and *higgledy-piggledy*. Words may be blended as in *blotch* from *blot* and *botch*, *blurt* from *blare* and *spurt*, *chump* from *chunk* and *lump*, *flaunt* from *flout* and *vaunt*, *flurry* from *fly* and *hurry*, *grumble* from *growl* and *rumble*, *splutter* from *splash* and *sputter*, and *twirl* from *twist* and *whirl*. By the most natural process in the world a word may by *aphesis* lose an initial unstressed syllable and assume a new meaning. Thus, for example, to *disport* oneself 'to carry oneself in a different direction from one's ordinary business' becomes *sport*; a *dispenser* 'a steward or butler who dispenses the household provisions' becomes *Spenser* or *Spencer*; *defend*, *defender*, and *defence* become, at different times and independently, *fend*, *fender*, and *fence*; *amend*, *attend*, *distain*, and *envy*, take on new ways as *mend*, *tend*, *stain*, and *vie*; *acute*, *alive* (on life), and *alone* (all one) give *cute*, *live* (as in 'live wire'), and *lone*; *assize*, *despite*, and *example* become *size*, *spite*, and *sample*. By the contrary process of *apocope* words may shed their final unstressed syllables. When people started calling a *cabriolet* a *cab* they showed a natural predilection for the snappy monosyllable. In colloquial speech they call a *perambulator* a *pram* and a *prefabricated house* a *prefab*. They go to the *Zoological Gardens* or the *Zoo* and to the *Promenade Concerts* or the *Proms*. Similarly a *chapman* has become a *chap* or 'merchant of any kind, good or bad', a *quacksalver* has become a *quack*, and a veterinary surgeon is affectionately referred to as a *vet*.

CHAPTER VIII

The Sentence

———————

WE do not learn to frame sentences instinctively, as we learn to breathe or to walk. We repeat sentences from memory and we vary them by analogy. Imagine for a moment that all the sentences you have uttered during the course of the last two weeks are somewhere accurately recorded and that you can now scrutinize them at leisure. You will probably find them to be surprisingly varied: long and short; simple, double, multiple, and complex; statements, commands, wishes, questions, and exclamations; balanced, periodic, and loose. The words have been largely of your own choosing, but the sentences have seldom been of your own making. You have inherited them from the immediate, the distant, and the long-distant past. You have carried with you in your mind a certain number of sentence-patterns, few or many according to your individual linguistic capacity, and into these patterns you have fitted and varied the words expressing your thoughts and desires.

A child may echo the sounds it hears without being conscious of the meanings of separate words. Because English is, in the main, an analytic language (in spite of reviving synthetic tendencies which we were considering in the last chapter), the sentence is the most important unit of English speech. The sentence is more important even than the word. Revelling in the exercise of its imitative faculty, a child will attempt, however imperfectly, to babble whole sentences. A schoolboy may be word-perfect in his recitation of a long and difficult poem while remaining blissfully ignorant of the poet's intention and meaning. 'If hopes were dupes, fears may be liars', I say to console a friend. He may like the words and repeat them, and yet neither of us may pause to reflect upon the astounding personifications implied by Clough in this oft-repeated line. 'Genuine poetry', Mr T. S. Eliot has reminded us, 'can communicate before it is understood'. A lovely sentence may haunt my memory –

> And I shall have some peace there, for peace comes dropping slow,
> Dropping from the veils of the morning to where the cricket sings

– and I may often murmur it to myself without being at all conscious of linguistic form, or function, or even of meaning. Nevertheless, the effective speaker and writer of prose is he who does not merely *catch* his sentence-patterns but who *grips* them and wields them with well-controlled purpose. In addition to possessing a ready command of vocabulary, the good speaker must be endowed with an unerring sense of rhythm. Even the most gifted orator, however, cannot depart too far from the speech patterns accepted by the community in which he lives without running the grave risk of being misapprehended or of being only partially understood. In ordinary affirmations the subject is followed by the predicate, consisting of verb and object or complement. In all the Indo-European languages the sentence is normally bipartite. Basically it is a two-in-one. It is a binary unit. The subject is that to which the speaker wishes to draw the hearer's attention and the predicate is that which the speaker has to say about that subject. If I utter a defective sentence it is probably because, for some reason or other, I have failed to keep these two things clear in my mind. In order to put it right, I have only to ask myself the simple questions: What am I talking about? What have I to say about it? Or, in other words: What is my subject? What do I predicate of that subject? As Edward Sapir has so well said (*Language*, p. 36), 'The major functional unit of speech, the sentence ... is the linguistic expression of a proposition. It combines a subject of discourse with a statement in regard to this subject. Subject and predicate may be combined in a single word, as in Latin *dico*; each may be expressed independently, as in the English equivalent, *I say*; each or either may be so qualified as to lead to complex propositions of many sorts. No matter how many of these qualifying elements (words or functional parts of words) are introduced, the sentence does not lose its feeling of unity so long as each and every one of them falls in place as contributory to the definition of either the subject of discourse or the core of the predicate.'

The predicate may indeed have preceded the subject in Proto-Indo-European, as in Modern Welsh, as in parenthetical 'said he', or as in H. G. Wells's stylistic mannerism 'Came a pause'. The sentence-type *Down came the rain*, which, as we have already seen in Chapter 5, is as old as Chaucer, finds its normal place in Modern German. Emphatic *down* comes first, the verb retains second place, and so the subject falls into the final position. It has been computed that the subject precedes the predicate in less than half of King Alfred's sentences, and if we study the shapes assumed by certain concrete locutions during the last thousand years or so, we detect a gradual shifting towards the modern order: subject, verb and object. Old English *mē gelīciaþ bēc* 'To me are pleasing books' becomes Modern English *I like books.* The vocables are identical, but the case of the pronoun has been altered from dative to nominative and the grammatical subject has been shifted from the things to the person. Since loving and liking are primarily active feelings, Modern English, it might be claimed, is here more rational than Old English. The modern grammatical subject becomes identical with the logical and the psychological one. Similarly, both *If you like* and *If you please* have derived historically from *If to you it may be pleasing* (*you* being dative of the pronoun and *like* and *please* third person singular of the present subjunctive) very much as in French *s'il vous plaît*, or Dutch *als 't u blieft* or old-fashioned German *wenn es Ihnen gefällt*, where, however, in all three languages, the verb is in the indicative. A still more striking example of the shifting of the grammatical subject to the first place in the sentence, without any resulting change in the position of the pronoun, is seen in *He was given the book* in which *the book* is 'retained object'. In the corresponding sentence in Old English, however, *the book* is the grammatical subject, *Him wæs gegiefen sēo bōc*, '(To) him was given the book'. Similarly Chaucer's *It am I*, in which the grammatical subject is *I* (Old English *Hit eom ic*, Latin *Ego sum*), becomes Modern English *It is I*. In Chaucer's day the subjective character of *I* was still so strong that, in spite of word order, *It am I* sounded just as natural as Old French *Ce suis je*. French has certainly gone further than English in normalizing *C'est moi*. 'L'état, c'est moi', said Louis XIV as long ago as in the seventeenth century, not 'L'état, c'est je'. *It is me* is regarded by many to be too colloquial for literary use. At the same time, the feeling predominates that, apart from grammatical structure, a verb should be followed by the accusative. No one, as Otto Jespersen pointed out, would venture to suggest changing Shelley's emphatic *me* in *Ode to the West Wind* –

> Be thou, Spirit fierce,
> My spirit! Be thou *me*, impetuous one!

No one is shocked by the ungrammatical *Fare thee well* instead of *Fare (go) thou well*.

In the sentence *It's me* the neuter pronoun *it* has no separate meaning. It is a meaningless substitute which brings this simple statement into the usual pattern of subject, verb, and complement. In the casual observations *It is blowing hard*, *It is cold*, and *It is raining*, you might too readily assume that the neuter pronoun stands for *the wind*, *the weather*, and *the rain* respectively. 'For the rain it raineth every day' sang the clown at the end of *Twelfth Night*, and Robert Louis Stevenson wrote playfully in his verses for children –

> The rain is raining all around
> It falls on field and tree.

After a little reflection you will probably conclude that *it* in *It is raining* is merely a substitute for the subject of the impersonal verb and that it expresses an action or a condition of things without reference to any agent.

Swift defined a good style as the use of proper words in proper places. The proper places will vary considerably according to degrees of emphasis. Usage has left many parts of the sentence relatively free and these we can vary to suit our purpose. Coleridge laid much stress on the importance of word order. He defined poetry, you may remember, as 'the best words in the best order'. In the words of the greatest poets 'there is', Coleridge asserted, 'a reason assignable not only for every word, but for the position of every word'. In the well-ordered sentence the hearer or the reader will receive no jolt or check. As Herbert Spencer observed, 'things which are to be thought of together must be mentioned as closely as possible together'. Naturally we place together such words as are more closely associated in meaning. We say 'a big brown dog' rather than 'a brown big dog', 'a handsome young man' and not 'a young handsome man', and 'a kind old gardener' and not 'an old kind gardener'. So, too, we place together those phrases which are most closely associated in our minds. 'Delighted to make your acquaintance' we say upon being introduced and not, as in German, 'Delighted your acquaintance to make'.

The classification of sentences is not a difficult matter. Sentences are of three kinds according to *form*: simple ('I know it'), compound ('I know it and I am proud of it'), and complex ('I know that he will come'). They are of four kinds according to *function*: statement ('I know it'), command-wish ('Long live the King!'), question ('Are you coming?'), and

xclamation ('How good you are!'). The verb generally
omes before the subject in wishes and questions. As we
ass from a simple to a complex sentence we do not, as
n some other languages, change the order of the words: 'I
hope (that) he will come. He will, I hope, come. Presumably
he will come.' But in German we are bound to say: 'Ich hoffe,
er wird kommen. Ich hoffe, dass er kommen wird. Hoffentlich
(vermutlich) wird er kommen.'

Sentences may be further categorized according to *style* as
loose, balanced, and periodic, although this division is of its
very nature somewhat vague and ill defined. All three types
of sentence are good and a master of English will weave them
skilfully into the varied fabric of style. In the so-called *loose*
sentence the writer or speaker states fact after fact just as these
occur to him, freely and artlessly. Daniel Defoe opens *The
Life and Adventures of Robinson Crusoe* with a long, loose, ram-
bling sentence which nevertheless grips our attention at once:
'I was born in the year 1632, in the city of York, of a good
family, though not of that country, my father being a
foreigner of Bremen, who settled first at Hull: he got a good
estate by merchandise, and leaving off his trade, lived after-
ward at York, from whence he had married my mother,
whose relations were named Robinson, a very good family
in that country, and from whom I was called Robinson
Kreutznoer; but, by the usual corruption of words in England,
we are now called, nay, we call ourselves, and write our name
Crusoe, and so my companions always called me.' The style is
conversational. We seem to hear the author talking quietly to
us in the first person and telling us the story of his life. This
imaginary autobiography seems at once factual and real. As
the writer tells us about the time and the place of his birth,
about his parentage and his name, he adds clause to clause
pleasantly. The sentence might well have ended after the first
clause, 'I was born in the year 1632'; or it might have ended
in at least thirteen other places after that. On the other hand,

it might have gone on and on for many pages. There is no
ambiguity, no obscurity, and no tautology. The reader re-
ceives no mental check. All is easy and natural. But behind
this apparent artlessness there is art concealed, and behind this
easy and natural prose – Defoe was writing in the year 1719 –
lay more than ten centuries of linguistic change and development. There is probably no surer way of appreciating the
maturity and concreteness of Defoe's prose than by translating
it into some foreign tongue.

In the *periodic* sentence the climax comes at the close. The
reader is held in suspense until at last he hears what he has long
been waiting for, and only then is he able to comprehend the
meaning of the sentence as a whole. It is a style cultivated to
good effect by the orators of classical antiquity, Demosthenes
and Cicero, as well as those of modern times, Burke and Gladstone. When, in *The Laws of Ecclesiasticall Politie*, Richard
Hooker reflected upon what might be the subsequent fate of
man if the ordinances of nature should fail, he expressed himself in a stately and sonorous prose far different from Defoe's:
'Now if nature should intermit her course, and leave altogether though it were but for a while the observation of her
own laws; if those principal and mother elements of the world,
whereof all things in this lower world are made, should lose
the qualities which now they have; if the frame of that
heavenly arch erected over our heads should loosen and dis-
solve itself; if celestial spheres should forget their wonted
motions, and by irregular volubility turn themselves any way
as it might happen; if the prince of the lights of heaven, which
now as a giant doth run his unwearied course, should as it were
through a languishing faintness begin to stand and to rest himself; if the moon should wander from her beaten way, the
times and seasons of the year blend themselves by disordered
and confused mixture, the winds breathe out their last gasp,
the clouds yield no rain, the earth be defeated of heavenly influence, the fruits of the earth pine away as children at the

withered breasts of their mother no longer able to yield them relief: what would become of man himself, whom these things now do all serve?' The language is highly rhythmical and the imagery is Biblical, reminiscent of Isaiah, the Psalms, and the Book of Job. The word-picture is painted with consummate art. After a long and steady climb upward over successive terraces of conditional clauses, the reader descends swiftly with the final rhetorical question.

As an example of a shorter but no less effective period we might consider the sentence in his *Autobiography* in which Edward Gibbon describes the birth of the idea of his great *History*: 'It was at Rome, on the 15th of October 1764, as I sat musing amidst the ruins of the Capitol, while the barefooted friars were singing vespers in the temple of Jupiter, that the idea of writing the decline and fall of the city first started to my mind.' In Rome, ruinous and Christian, late in the afternoon in the fall of the year, the inspiration came to the historian. The word-picture is brief, but it is artistically perfect. The rhythm is stately and entirely satisfying. The reader is held in suspense to the end.

Had he wished, and had he been less of an artist, Gibbon might have said exactly the same things in a different way, arranging them in their logical and grammatical order: 'The idea of writing the decline and fall of the city first started to my mind as I sat musing amidst the ruins of the Capitol at Rome on the 15th of October 1764, while the barefooted friars were singing vespers in the temple of Jupiter.' What has happened? It is not merely that a periodic sentence has been re-expressed as a loose one. The emphasis is now all wrong and the magnificent cadence of the original is quite marred. All is still grammatically correct, but 'proper words' are no longer in 'proper places'. The passage has quite lost its harmonious rhythm.

The *balanced* sentence satisfies a profound human desire for equipoise and symmetry and it has long been at home in

4

English as in Hebrew, Greek, and Latin, and many other languages both ancient and modern. It may express two similar thoughts in *parallelism* or two opposing ones in *antithesis*. Such proverbial sayings as *Like master like man*, *More haste less speed*, *First come first served*, and *Least said soonest mended* probably represent a primitive Indo-European sentence-type which survives in many lands.

'Children sweeten labours', wrote Francis Bacon, 'but they make misfortunes more bitter: they increase the cares of life, but they mitigate the remembrance of death'. Speaking at the Guildhall, London, on November 9, 1805, just one fortnight after the Battle of Trafalgar, William Pitt declared: ' England has saved herself by her exertions and will, I trust, save Europe by her example'. No less memorable was the balanced sentence uttered in the House of Lords by Edward Viscount Grey of Fallodon on August 3, 1914, on the eve of Britain's entry into the First World War: 'The lamps are going out all over Europe: we shall not see them lit again in our lifetime.'

English sentence-patterns show infinite variety and *loose*, *periodic*, and *balanced* are only relative terms. The best writers shape their sentences in such a way as to give just the right degree of emphasis, and this they must achieve, in written language, by word order alone. Now it is certainly not surprising that in a language like ours, with such a long history behind it, some patterns have become blended, mixed, or, to use the technical term, 'contaminated', and that some of these 'contaminations' have been sanctioned by usage. 'I am friendly with him' and 'We are friends' ('He and I are friends') have become contaminated and so have produced 'I am friends with him'. It is an idiom or manner of expression peculiar to English. 'I am friends with him' cannot be translated literally into French, German, or Italian, though it is as old as Shakespeare. 'I am good friends with my father', says Prince Hal (I *Henry the Fourth*, III. iii. 202), 'and may do any thing'.

'But whom say ye that I am?' (*St Matthew*, XVI, 15) is frequently quoted from the King James Bible as an example of an ungrammatical accusative *whom* used as the complement of the verb *to be*. Is it, then, an error? Perhaps no direct yes or no can be given in answer to this question. The sentence is a good example of a blending of 'Who say ye that I am?' and 'Whom say ye me to be?' That is all. The English poets, even the very greatest of them, have occasionally indulged in such contaminations of sentence-structures, refusing to be bound by strict rules. 'I should have liked to have been there', some-one will say. Clearly this is a blending of 'I should like (I wish now as I look back) to have been there' and 'I should have liked (but unfortunately I was unable) to be there'. 'They each did their best' is likewise a mixture of 'They all (all of them) did their best' and 'Each of them did his best'.

If it is true that we repeat sentences from memory and vary them by analogy, and that we do not really frame sentences in any other way, then we should perhaps look upon all analo-gous creations with a kind and indulgent eye. 'Do like I do' is no worse than Elizabethan 'Do like as I do'. 'Do like me' and 'Do as I do' mark a desirable distinction, but it would be well to recognize that that distinction is more stylistic than gram-matical. 'What are you doing of?' is the Cockney's analogous creation, based upon 'What are you doing?' and 'What are you thinking of?' 'I would say' and 'I should like to say' are blended and so we hear 'I would like to say', an undesirable form which is helped on its way to acceptance by the general tendency, especially in North America and in Ireland, to ignore the (relatively recent) traditional distinctions between *shall* (*should*) in the first person and *will* (*would*) in the second and third. 'It looks as though' is now on everyone's lips – 'It looks as though there will be a general election (or anything else for that matter) soon.' 'It looks to me', said Burke in 1790 (*Reflections on the Revolution in France*) 'as if I were in a great crisis'. The verb to-day would be in the past subjunctive (or subjunctive equivalent) if people were conscious of the precise implication: 'It appears as would or might be the case if'. But 'It looks as though' has come to be a mere substitute for 'apparently, probably, by all appearances', and it is now invariably followed by the future tense. 'You and I will decide between us' has influenced 'Let you and me decide' which becomes 'Let you and I decide' on the lips of the heedless, who no longer think of 'Let us decide' as 'Allow us to decide' supplanting 'Decide we', the old jussive. Whatever the grammarians may say, there is abundant evidence in many languages for the use of the superlative degree in a comparison of only two persons or things. Nevertheless, 'Which (selective) is the stronger of the two?' is more satisfactory than 'Who is the strongest of the two?' If we say 'He was one of the kindest men that has ever lived' we break that favourite rule of the prescriptive grammarians which states that the verb in a relative clause should agree with its nearer antecedent. Doubtless we are thereby confusing 'He was the kindest man that ever lived' and 'He was one of the kindest men that have ever lived'. We may confuse 'The reason why printing is slow is that paper is scarce' and 'Printing is slow because paper is scarce' and, as a result, we say 'The reason why printing is slow is because paper is scarce'. If we are observant and alert, we shall probably hear many interesting 'contaminations', such as these, both tolerable and intolerable, every day of our lives.

Another interesting thing we shall observe is the way in which natural emphasis overrides strict logic in word order. 'He only died last week' may be denounced by modern precisians on the ground that it flouts one of those rules of proximity whereby the modifying adverb should be placed as near as possible to the word, phrase or clause it modifies. 'He died only last week' or 'It was only last week that he died' should stand. Stress, intonation, and pause, however, make everything clear, or even clearer, when *only* is detached. 'He only died last week' implies no ambiguity and no misplaced emphasis. Shakespeare himself wrote in Sonnet XCIV –

> The summer's flower is to the summer sweet
> Though to itself it only live and die

– and not 'Though only to itself' or 'Though to itself alone', the latter cadence seeming certainly preferable to my modern ear. Mr Vernon Bartlett once opened a wireless talk on world affairs with the words: 'I am not an expert on China. I have only been there twice in my life'. Natural emphasis and intonation were just right: the hearer's attention was arrested at once. 'I have been there only twice in my life' would have sounded unnatural and pedantic in comparison. Language, after all, is more psychological than logical. So, too, in regard to the placing of the preposition, we should do well to divest ourselves of the notion that it is 'an inelegant word to end a sentence with' and that, just because it is called a *pre-position*, it must therefore 'be placed before'. In Old English (*ūs betwēonan* 'between us') as in Latin (*pāx vōbiscum* 'peace be with you'), there were *postpositions* and the tradition has been kept alive through centuries of English poetry: 'the table round' (Shakespeare); 'stoutly struts his dames before' (Milton); 'my heart within' (Scott); 'the willowy hills and fields among' (Tennyson); 'I will go to France again, and tramp the valley through' (Flecker). The final preposition became a butt for the nineteenth-century grammarians, who averred that the most careful writers avoided it and that the Authorized Version of the Bible contained not one instance of it. As a matter of fact, the curious reader will not go far in the Book of Genesis before encountering an example in Chapter XXVIII: 'I will not leave thee, until I have done that which I have spoken to thee of'. It is a remarkable fact that even Dryden, that acknowledged master of English prose, criticized Ben Jonson's conversational style adversely on the ground that it showed the 'common fault' of putting the preposition at the end, a fault which, Dryden added, 'I have but lately observed in my own writings'. Indeed, when revising his *Essay of Dramatic Poesy*, Dryden went so far as to rewrite the sentences in which an end preposition occurred and his illustrious example was followed by others. To-day we accept the final preposition as permissible and desirable in such natural and spontaneous expressions as 'What are you thinking of?' and 'I sometimes wonder what the world is coming to'. Phrasal verbs, consisting of verbs joined with adverbs and prepositions, are now in such frequent use that, in order to avoid the prepositional ending entirely, a speaker would sometimes be driven to perpetrate an intolerably artificial sentence. Against such a clumsy sentence, according to Sir Ernest Gowers (*Plain Words*, p. 74), Sir Winston Churchill is said to have added the marginal comment: 'This is the sort of English up with which I will not put'. Sir Ernest goes on to tell the story of a nurse who contrived to get no fewer than four prepositions together at the end of a sentence when she asked a child: 'What did you choose that book to be read to out of for?' And did the child understand? If stress, rhythm, intonation, and pause were right, yes. The nurse 'said what she wanted to say perfectly clearly, in words of one syllable, and what more can one ask?' You may have observed, by the way, that *out* in 'read to out of for' is really an adverb or, if you will, that *out-of* is a prepositional compound consisting of adverb and preposition. At any rate, the dividing line between prepositions and adverbs is often shadowy and vague.

The English sentence, then, is something of a paradox. Word order has become more significant than hitherto, far more important than in Old, Middle, or Tudor English, and yet it has retained enough of its elasticity to give to the skilful speaker all the scope and power he needs. We English have inherited our sentence-patterns, but we have abundant freedom to vary words, phrases, and clauses within those inherited patterns. We shall be effective as speakers and as writers if we can say clearly, simply, and attractively just what we want to say and nothing more. If we really have something worth saying, then we are bound by the nature and necessities of our language to say it as simply as ever we can. If we have something very abstruse and complex to say, then, of course, we cannot say it simply, but we shall endeavour to say it as clearly as the theme permits. We shall vary our style, our vocabulary and our speech-level to suit the occasion and, at the same time, we shall never lose sight of the needs and capacities of our hearers. If, following the wise counsel of Aristotle, we keep these three things constantly in mind – our subject-matter, our purpose, and our audience – all will be well.

CHAPTER IX

Etymology and Meaning

_____

FEW words have fixed significations like the pure numbers of mathematics or the technical formulas of chemistry. The mathematical sign π denotes a constant, namely, the ratio of the circumference of a circle to its diameter, or $3.14159\ldots$ The chemical formula NaCl denotes a substance, sodium chloride, or salt, and it always means that substance and nothing else. These symbols π and NaCl cannot vary with time or circumstance, nor do they ever change with their contexts. Few expressions in daily use have such simple and direct denotations as these. Even words like _mother_ and _father_, _sun_ and _horse_, denoting primary human relationships or natural objects and creatures, are not quite so definite. All four words occur in Old English and their meanings have not changed in twelve centuries. But in such sayings as 'Westminster is the mother of Parliaments', 'The child is father of the man', 'He seeks a place in the sun', and 'He rides the high horse', the primary meanings of these words are manifestly transcended.

What is the _sun_? According to _The Oxford English Dictionary_ it is 'the brightest (as seen from the earth) of the heavenly bodies, the luminary or orb of day; the central body of the solar system, around which the earth and other planets revolve, being kept in their orbits by its attraction and supplied with light and heat by its radiation'. And what is the _horse_? It is 'a solid-hoofed perissodactyl quadruped (_Equus caballus_), having a flowing mane and tail, whose voice is a neigh'. Now are these so-called 'dictionary definitions' really definitions, or are they not descriptions? As long ago as 1891, when he was writing his magistral *Essai de Sémantique*, Michel Bréal demonstrated that the cause of shifting meaning in so many words lay in the impossibility of complete definition and in the varying complexity of the word-thing relationship. 'Language', he wrote, 'designates things in an incomplete and inaccurate manner: *incomplete*, since we have not exhausted all that can be said of the sun when we have declared it to be shining, or of the horse when we say that it trots; *inaccurate*, since we cannot say of the sun that it shines when it has set, or of the horse that it trots when it is at rest, or when it is wounded or dead.'

Could the word or symbol *sun* ever alter its reference and come to mean 'moon', or 'star', or something else? That, surely, is inconceivable. *Sun* is an ancient word, indicating the same 'heavenly body' as its ancestral equivalent in Indo-European five thousand and more years ago. Day by day during those five thousand years, man has observed it 'coming forth as a bridegroom out of his chamber, and rejoicing as a giant to run his course'. Nevertheless, it has happened that üλ, the etymological equivalent of *sun* in Albanian (with *l* - instead of *n* - formative), has come to mean 'star'; whereas *súil*, its counterpart in Erse, has come to mean 'eye'. At some period in the history of each of these two languages that apparently simple and rigid relationship between word and thing, between *symbol* and *referend*, has been deflected and distorted. The meaning, we say, has been changed. The seemingly impossible has occurred and any notions that we may have entertained concerning the indissolubility of the links connecting *etymology* and *meaning* have been rudely dispelled. The shock is, to say the least, disconcerting. We should so much prefer to regard a 'speech-form as a relatively permanent object to which the meaning is attached as a kind of changeable satellite' (Leonard Bloomfield, *Language*, p. 426). The study of language would be so much easier for us if we could be assured that the etymology of a word is not only something *real* and *true* (as, indeed, the Greek *etymon* implies) but also that it is something permanent; and that the basic form or *root* of a word has some inherent connexion with the thing, quality or action denoted. Primitive peoples still believe that word has power over thing, that somehow the word participates of the nature of the thing. The word, in fact, is the symbol and it has no direct or immediate relation with the referend except through the image in the mind of the speaker. As Henri Delacroix once said (in *Le Langage et la Pensée*), 'All thought is symbolic. Thought first constructs symbols which it substitutes for things.' The symbol *sun* has no connexion with the celestial luminary other than through the thoughts or images in the mind of the speaker and the hearer. Unless these two images are identical, there can be no complete understanding.

Latin grammarians sometimes taught wrong etymologies long ago and more recent writers, who should have known better, have occasionally had recourse to fictitious etymologies in order to buttress a theory or to point a moral. Carlyle liked to define *king* as 'he who can', associating the word with German *können* 'to be capable, to know how to'; and Ruskin found pleasure in reminding the married women in his audience that since *wife* meant 'she who weaves', their place was in the home. On the other hand, a speaker may knowingly or unwittingly ignore an etymology. He may refer to a 'dilapidated wooden shed', although *dilapidated* is strictly applicable only to a building of stone (Latin *lapis, lapidis*). He may say that 'the battalion was well equipped', although *to equip* (French *équiper*, from Old Norse *skipa*) means historically 'to fit out a ship'. He may say that 'the life-boat was manned by Wrens', 'the ocean liner sailed', and 'the cattle were shepherded into their stables'. A rediscovered etymology may be highly informative and may give pleasure. Those two attractive birds, the nuthatch and the redstart, have most interesting names. The nuthatch is that little creeping bird that breaks or *hacks* the nuts in order to feed on the kernel. For the alternation between final plosive and affricative in *hack* and *hatch*, you may like to compare *bake* and *batch*, *dike* and *ditch*, *lyke*wake and *lich*gate, *mickle* and *much*, *wake* and *watch*. The redstart is still called the fire-tail in some dialects and *start* 'tail' survives in *Start* Point 'tail-shaped promontory' and *stark*-naked, older *start*-naked. It is interesting to recall that a *governor* is etymologically a 'steersman', a *marshal* a 'horse-servant', and a *constable* a 'companion of the stable'. A *companion* is 'one who eats bread' with another, a *fellow* is 'one who lays down money', a *comrade* a 'chamber-fellow', and a *friend* 'one who loves'.

If the meanings of words are not fixed, if they are liable to flux and change, is there any way of predicting in which direction they are most likely to change? Do changes in meaning admit of empirical generalizations? It is the aim of students of *semantics* or *semasiology* to find the answers to these questions. So far there has been little co-ordination of semantic research and investigators have fallen into two groups according to their preoccupation with mental processes (Bronislaw Malinowski, C. K. Ogden, and I. A. Richards) or with mathematical symbols (Ludwig Wittgenstein, A. N. Whitehead, Bertrand Russell, and Rudolf Carnap). At present these two groups – the linguistic psychologists and the mathematical logicians – seem to be moving on different planes. The student of language sees many parallels, and he is able to distinguish certain semantic categories, but he inclines to the view that generalizations are dangerous and unprofitable.

The most obvious semantic category is that involving specialization or narrowing. When a speech-form is applied to a group of objects or ideas which resemble one another in some respect, it may naturally become restricted to just one object or idea, and if this particular restriction gains currency in a speech community, a specialized meaning prevails. *Meat*, as in *sweetmeat* and as in the archaic phrase 'meat and drink', meant any kind of food. It now means 'edible flesh', a sense formerly expressed by *flesh* and *flesh meat*. *Deer*, like Dutch *dier* and German *Tier*, used to mean 'animal' in general, as in Shakespeare's 'mice and rats and such small deer'. Latin *animal* and French *beast* have taken its place as the general words and *deer* now means 'wild ruminant of a particular (antlered) species'. *Fowl*, like Dutch and German *Vogel*, denoted 'bird in general' as in Chaucer's 'Parlement of Foules' and Biblical 'fowls of the air' and as in modern names of larger kinds of birds used with a qualifying adjective, such as *sea fowl*, *water fowl*, and *wild fowl*. Otherwise, of course, *fowl* normally means a domestic cock or hen, especially when full grown. *Hound* formerly meant a dog of any breed and not, as now, a hunting-dog in particular. *Disease* was still conceived in Chaucer's day as being dis-ease 'absence of ease'. It might point to any kind of temporary discomfort and not, as now, to 'a morbid physical condition'. To *starve*, like Dutch *sterven* and German *sterben*, meant 'to die', not necessarily from lack of food. In modern Yorkshire dialect a body can still 'starve of cold'. A *wed* was a pledge of any kind. In conjunction with the suffix *-lock* forming nouns of action, it has come to be restricted to 'the marriage vow or obligation'. To the Elizabethans an *affection* was a feeling of any kind and both *lectures* and *lessons* were 'readings' of any kind. *Doctrine* was still teaching in general and *science* was still knowledge in general.

Sometimes a word has become restricted in use because a qualifier has been omitted. *Undertaker*, like French *entrepreneur* and German *Unternehmer*, used to mean 'contractor, one who *undertakes* to do a particular piece of work'. It is now used exclusively in the sense of *funeral undertaker*, although *mortician* has already superseded it in the cities and towns of America. In daily conversation *doctor* 'teacher' means 'medical doctor' and normally refers to a 'general practitioner'. Many words have both wider and narrower senses in the living language and many others have varying senses according to the persons addressed. *Pipe*, for example, evokes different images in the mind of the smoker, the plumber, the civil engineer, the geologist, the organist, and the boatswain. The *line* means a clothes-line to the laundrywoman, a fishing line to the fisherman, the equator to the seaman (as in Joseph Conrad's *Crossing the Line*), a communication wire to the telephonist, a succession of descent to the genealogist, and a particular kind of article to the man of business. To the geographer *cataract* means a cascade or waterfall, to the engineer a hydraulic controller, but a disease of the crystalline lens to the oculist.

The processes of specialization and extension of meaning may take place in a language side by side. For instance, as we have just seen, *hound* has been restricted in the course of a thousand years from a dog in general to a hunting-dog in particular; contrariwise, *dog*, which we encountered as an eleventh-century *ex nihilo* word in Chapter 7, has been extended from 'a dog of ancient breed' to include any sort of dog, ranging from a formidable Alsatian to a puny and insignificant lap-dog. *Bird* meant 'young birdling', just as *pigeon* meant 'young dove' and *pig* 'young swine'. *Place* has had a remarkable history in English, where it has largely superseded the older words *stead* and *stow*. It derives from the feminine form of the Greek adjective meaning 'broad', as in *plateîa hodós* 'broad way'. In one of its senses it still means 'a group of houses in a town or city, now or formerly possessing some of the characters (positive or negative) of a square', like its well-known cognate in French, as in *Place de la Concorde*, or like Italian *piazza*, Spanish *plaza*, and German *Platz*. Now, however, it is also used in a hundred ways: 'Keep him in his place', 'It is not my place to inquire into that', 'The meeting will not take place', 'There is a place for everything', 'I have lost the place (in reading)', 'That remark was quite out of place (inappropriate, improper)', 'In the first, second place (first, secondly)'.

If we assume that the central meaning of *place* is still 'square' and that these other diverse uses *radiate* from that centre, we might equally well put it into our third semantic category: radiation, polysemia, or multiplication. Another excellent example is the word *paper*. It is the same as *papyrus*, the paper-reed of the Nile from the thin strips of which writing-sheets were first made as a substitute for parchment. The name was naturally transferred to paper made of cotton and thence to paper of linen and other fibres. To-day a paper may mean a document of any kind, for instance, a Government White Paper; an essay, dissertation or article on some particular topic, especially a communication read or sent to a learned society; a set of questions in an examination; a journal or a daily newspaper. *Power* 'ability to do, state of being able' may hold radiating meanings as diverse as 'capacity for mental or bodily action' (power of intellect, power of movement); 'mechanical or natural energy' (horse-power, candle-power, electric power-station); 'political or national strength' (the balance of power); 'possession of control or command over others, dominion, sway' (the power of the Cabinet); 'a political state' (the four great powers); and 'a mathematical conception' (5^4 or five to the fourth power). Because the *head* is that part of the human body containing the brain, it may be the top of anything, literally or metaphorically, whether it resembles the head in shape (the head of a nail, screw, pin, hammer, walking-stick, flower, or cabbage) or in position (the head of the page, the list, the bed, the table or the stairs); or it may signify the person who is the chief or leader (the head of the school, the business, the family, the house, the State, the Church). It may denote the head of a coin (that side of a coin bearing the sovereign's head); a headland or promontory (St Bees Head, Great Ormes Head, or Beachy Head, from tautologous Beau Chef Head); a single person or beast (lunch at five shillings a head, fifty head of cattle); or one of the main points or logical divisions of a subject or discourse (dealing with a theme under several heads). These and other senses do not derive from one another. They radiate from a common centre and are therefore mutually independent. Some of these senses will be translated by German *Kopf*, by French *tête*, by Spanish *cabeza* or by the ordinary word for *head* in other languages, but many senses will not permit of such direct translation. Each sense must be considered separately and, in the process of translating, our linguistic knowledge may be severely put to the test. It is surprising that in ordinary conversation in English there is so little ambiguity.

It is surprising, too, that every day we use words in both literal and metaphorical senses and that there is little danger of being misapprehended. We may speak as we will of 'bright sunshine' or 'a bright boy'; 'a sharp knife', 'a sharp frost' or 'a sharp rebuke'; 'a cold morning' or 'the cold war'; 'the Black Country' or 'the black market'. A person who is slow-witted may be described metaphorically as 'dull', 'obtuse', or 'dim', the latter term being associated with the German *dumm* meaning 'stupid', although cognate with our *dumb*. 'Dumb' in German is now *stumm*, which is related etymologically to our *stammer*. Many words are themselves old metaphors: *dependent* 'hanging from' (Latin *dē-pendens*); *egregious* 'selected from the herd' (Latin *ē* for *ex* + *grex, gregis* 'herd'); *precocious* 'too early ripe' (Latin *praecox* from *prae* 'before' + *coquere* 'to cook, ripen').

Our next category of semantic changes may be labelled concretization. The naming of abstract qualities, such as *whiteness*, *beauty*, and *justice*, comes late in the evolution of a language because it results from conscious or unconscious comparison in the mind of man. Does *beauty* really exist apart from beautiful things? On this question the medieval school-men argued for centuries. No sooner are abstract nouns formed than men tend to think of each appearance of a quality or action in the abstract as a separate entity and so, by concretization, they make abstractions tangible and visible once more. *Youth*, 'youngness' in the abstract, becomes a 'young man'. In the form *geogoþ* this word occurs eleven times in *Beowulf*, five times with the abstract meaning 'youth', but six times with the concrete and collective meaning 'young men'. In much the same way Latin *multitūdo* 'manyness, the quality of being many' came to signify 'a crowd' and *congregātio* 'flocking together' came to mean 'a body of people assembled'. Barristers appointed counsel to the Crown are named *King's Counsel*. A judge is addressed as *Your Honour* and an archbishop as *Your Grace*. *Health* is the quality of being *hale* or *whole*, soundness of body and mind. Modern man seeks diligently to maintain physical, mental, and social health. It is Greek *hugíeia* (from the adjectival form of which comes our *hygiene*), Latin *salūs*, French *la santé*, and German *die Gesundheit*. Clearly these are all highly abstract forms. Nevertheless, even *health* becomes concrete in the sense of a toast drunk – 'Here's a health unto His Majesty!' *Wealth* was primarily 'weal', 'welfare', or 'well-being', the state of being 'well'. In the old assonantal formula 'health and wealth' the two abstract substantives were practically synonymous. But side by side with this meaning of *wealth* the concretized sense of 'worldly goods, riches, affluence' also developed. The expression *wealth of nations*, denoting 'the collective riches of a people or country', was certainly current before it was adopted by Adam Smith in 1776 as the title of his epoch-making book. 'Money', wrote John Stuart Mill in 1848, 'being the instrument of an important public and private purpose, is rightly regarded as wealth'. 'Let us substitute welfare for wealth as our governing purpose', said Edward Hallett Carr in 1948, exhorting us, in fact, to restore to the word *wealth* its older meaning. *Kindness, mercy, opportunity*, and *propriety* are historically abstractions, but to-day we speak of *kindnesses* in the plural in the sense of 'deeds of kindness', *mercies* as 'instances or manifestations of mercy', *opportunities* as 'favourable chances or occasions', and *proprieties* as 'proper forms of conduct'. Similarly *provision* 'foreseeing, foresight' has come to be applied in the plural to 'stores of food'.

Sometimes words, like men, 'fall away from their better selves' and show deterioration or catachresis. *Silly* once meant 'happy, blissful, holy', as in the 'sely child' of Chaucer's *Prioress's Tale*. Later it signified 'helpless, defenceless', becoming a conventional epithet in the 'silly sheep' of Milton, Cowper, and Matthew Arnold. Then it descended yet lower and came to imply 'foolish, feeble-minded, imbecile'. *Crafty* 'strong' and *cunning* 'knowing' were once attributes of unmingled praise. A crafty workman was one skilled in a handicraft; a cunning workman was one who knew his trade. *To counterfeit* meant simply 'to copy, reproduce', conveying no suggestion of fraud. 'What finde I here?' asked Bassanio, as he opened the leaden casket, 'Faire Portias counterfeit.' (*The Merchant of Venice*, III, ii, 115.) It was, in fact, no counterfeit in the modern sense, but a true and lifelike delineation that came 'so near creation'. A *villain* once meant 'a slave serving in a country-house or *villa*', a man occupying a lowly station in life. Chaucer's *vileynye* already showed depreciation, for it connoted the opposite of *courteisye*, that comprehensive term for a noble and chivalrous way of life, implying high courtly elegance and politeness of manners. A *knave*, like German *ein Knabe*, was just 'a boy'; later, as in 'the kokes knave, thet wassheth the disshes' of the *Ancrene Riwle*, 'a boy or lad employed as a servant'; later still, 'a base and crafty rogue'. Like *rogue* and *rascal*, *knave* may still be used jocularly without seriously implying bad qualities. *Varlet*, a variant of *valet*, has shown an almost identical catachresis. *Nice* has become just a pleasant verbal counter: anything or everything may be nice. But *nescius*, its Latin antecedent, had the precise meaning 'ignorant, unaware', a meaning maintained in Chaucer side by side with that of 'foolish'. From 'foolish' it developed the sense 'foolishly particular about small things', and so 'fastidious, precise', as in 'nice in one's dress'. Later it was made to refer to actions or qualities, as in 'a nice discrimination' and 'a nice sense of honour'. Since then, as H. W. Fowler has sagaciously observed in *A Dictionary of Modern English Usage*, 'it has been too great a favourite with the ladies, who have charmed out of it all its individuality and converted it into a mere diffuser of vague and mild agreeableness'. It is a pleasant, lazy word which careful speakers are bound to avoid using in serious contexts. *Propaganda*, which now implies an organized and vicious distortion of facts for a particular purpose, has suffered sad depreciation in recent years. In 1622 Pope Gregory XV founded a special Committee or Congregation of Cardinals for the Propagation of the Faith, in Latin *Congregātio dē propāgandā fide*. That marked the beginning of the history of this word, which, you see, is the ablative singular feminine form of the gerundive of *propāgāre* 'to fasten or peg down slips of plants for growth, to multiply plants by layering'. Most appropriately the Latin metaphor is agricultural and botanical. *Propaganda* should mean, in its extended sense, the dissemination of news of any kind. Unfortunately, since the year 1880 the meaning of the word has been poisoned. Propaganda and trustworthy news are dissociated in our minds. We even hear of propaganda and counter-propaganda!

Now all these semantic categories – specialization, extension, radiation, metaphor, concretization, and deterioration – are very interesting. Others too might be added to show in yet greater detail how inconstant are the relationships between symbol, image, and referend (word, thought, and thing). Men have sometimes associated speech-forms wrongly and the meanings of words have thus been modified capriciously and unpredictably. Let us admit that there have been losses and gains. When we blunder and are forced to offer abject apologies, we talk of eating *humble pie* and not *umble pie*, one made of umbles or entrails. Vaguely and hazily we may associate the epithet with *humble bee*, which is the old *hummle bee*, the bee that continuously *hums*. Hazily and lazily we may associate an *insurance policy* with the Government's *foreign policy*, not pausing to recollect that these two *policies* are etymologically quite different words. We associate *touchy* with *to touch*, forgetting that *touchy*, *techy*, or *tetchy* derives from *tetch* 'a fit of petulance or anger, a tantrum'. We say *restive* 'refusing to move or budge' when we are half thinking of *restless*. Pardonably, perhaps, we connect *uproar* with *roar* and *outrage* with *rage*.

Certain expressions, like *comity* and *fruition*, are frequently 'used loosely', and, since they are correspondingly in danger of being 'understood loosely' too, careful speakers are almost compelled to refrain from using them. *Comity* means 'courtesy, urbanity', not 'company, assembly'. The *comity of nations* is 'the obligation recognized by civilized nations to respect one another's laws and customs'. *Fruition* signifies 'enjoyment', not 'bearing of fruit'. 'If we live by hope', said Bishop Hugh Latimer, 'let us desire the end and fruition of our hope'. Like Archbishop Thomas Cranmer in the Epiphany Collect, Latimer was here using the word correctly. To-day we frequently hear of plans and projects 'coming, or being brought, to fruition'. *Definitive* 'having the quality or character of finality' should not be used as a more imposing form of *definite* 'clear, precise, unmistakable'. Our conception of the Middle Ages may be given a rosy tinge by an over-optimistic misinterpretation of the phrase 'merry England', echoed by Sir Walter Scott in the opening sentence of *Ivanhoe*. King Charles II was 'the merry monarch' and fun-fairs have their 'merry-go-rounds', but 'merry England' implied a pleasant and delightful countryside rather than a gay and carefree people. It was in the Northern *Cursor Mundi* that this epithet was first applied specifically to England. Later medieval poets repeated it and Spenser gave it wide currency in the First Book of *The Faerie Queene* (Canto X, Stanza 61) when he identified the Red Cross Knight with 'Saint George of mery England'. But Spenser's 'mery England' in the sixteenth century meant

much the same as Blake's 'England's green and pleasant land'
in the early nineteenth.

When Francis Bacon referred to various people in the course
of his *Essays* as *indifferent*, *obnoxious*, and *officious*, he was
describing them as 'impartial', 'submissive', and 'ready to serve'.
When King James II observed that the new St Paul's Cathedral
was *amusing*, *awful*, and *artificial*, he implied that Sir Christo-
pher Wren's recent creation was 'pleasing, awe-inspiring, and
skilfully achieved'. When Dr Johnson averred that Milton's
Lycidas was *easy*, *vulgar*, and therefore *disgusting*', he intended
to say that it was 'effortless, popular, and therefore not in good
taste'.

Men frequently find themselves at cross-purposes with one
another because they persist in using words in different senses.
Their long arguments emit more heat than light because their
conceptions of the point at issue, whether Marxism, democracy, capitalism, the good life, western civilization, culture,
art, internationalism, freedom of the individual, equality of
opportunity, redistribution of wealth, social security, progress, or what not, are by no means identical. From heedless-
ness, sloth, or sheer lack of intelligence men do not trouble to
clarify their conceptions. Symbols or counters remain unchanged, but as the argument proceeds images and referends
(thoughts and things) vary without end. By the way, what do
you mean by *progress*? To define your terms at every step may
seem an intolerable burden, but it is a sobering and salutary
discipline. It is, indeed, the only effective way to sharpen up a
blunted word and to restore its cutting edge.

CHAPTER X

Authority and Usage

WHY has England no authoritative linguistic academy, like the Italian *Accademia della Crusca* (1582) or the *Académie française* (1635), which might give clear and definite rulings on such vexatious questions as the split infinitive, the fused participle, the final preposition, double comparison and accumulation of negatives; and which might state unequivocally whether such oft-repeated expressions as 'Go slow', 'the three alternatives', 'between four walls', 'It's no use complaining', 'I didn't use to go', 'Who do you mean?' and 'It's me', are acceptable English or not? After all, general counsels – 'Remember that good English follows clear thinking', or 'Have something to say and try hard to say it' – are not particularly helpful when we are halting between two expressions and are in need of guidance. In daily conversation and in small talk we may not worry much about precision, but when we have to address a critical audience in public or when we have to present a formal report or record, we are not content with second best.

Although England has no Academy quite like the Italian and French Academies, there are various public bodies which concern themselves with language, and these include the British Academy, the Philological Society, the English Association, and the Committee on Spoken English of the British Broadcasting Corporation. The British Academy resembles the French Academy more in name than in fact. Incorporated as a learned society in the year 1902, it now comprises one hundred and fifty regular and forty-five corresponding Fellows. It meets regularly at Burlington House in Piccadilly. The British Academy claims to promote 'the study of the moral and political sciences, including history, philosophy, law, political economy, archaeology, and philology'. Eminent philologists like Dr Henry Bradley and Sir William Craigie have been included among its Fellows, but whatever pronouncements on good English they may have uttered from time to time have been made by them as individuals, and not as Academicians. So far as I know, the British Academy has never attempted to give authoritative advice on any linguistic question.

The Philological Society meets regularly in London, sometimes in Oxford and Cambridge, and occasionally in one of the Northern Universities. It was organized in its present form in 1842 with an initial membership of about two hundred persons, who met together with the professed object of 'investigating the structure, affinities, and history of language', but who early embarked upon two projects which were destined to be of great significance for the study of English, namely, the compilation of a Dictionary and the editing of hitherto unpublished texts in Old and Middle English. The first project was launched in the autumn of 1857 by Dr Richard Chenevix Trench, then Dean of Westminster, later Archbishop of Dublin, when he read two papers to the Society on the need of a new English Dictionary. Trench was already well known to the general public by his attractive little books on *English Past and Present* and *The Study of Words*. His suggestions were carried into effect two years later, when Herbert Coleridge (1830–1861), great-nephew of Samuel Taylor Coleridge, began work as first general editor. He continued until his untimely death, when he was succeeded by Frederick James Furnivall (1825–1910), who also founded *The Early English Text Society* in fulfilment of the founders' second project to make the older literature available to the dictionary-makers in competent editions. As we shall see later in this chapter, the Philological Society's Dictionary is universally recognized to be the highest authority on the use of the English language. To-day the Society professes 'to investigate and to promote the study and knowledge of the structure, the affinities, and the history of languages'. It does not lay claim to any authority or to any supervisory powers.

The English Association, founded in 1906, is a society of unrestricted membership which seeks, by means of lectures, readings, discussions, conferences, and publications, 'to unite and introduce to one another those who are interested in English Language and Literature, whether as writers, teachers, artists, actors, or administrators; and ... to uphold the standard of English writing and speech'. Its headquarters are in London, but it has branches all over the Commonwealth. It is a link between universities and schools and it enables the general public to meet and hear eminent poets and men of letters; it encourages younger writers to publish their work. The Association's officers give generous advice and help on many matters concerned with the fostering of good English, but they neither seek nor hold any kind of literary or linguistic authority.

In the early days of broadcasting the B.B.C. Advisory Committee on Spoken English was constituted 'to help those whose daily duty it is to broadcast the world's news'. It began its work in 1926, consisting of six members under the chairmanship of the Poet Laureate, Robert Bridges. In 1934 the Committee was enlarged and Bernard Shaw was elected Chairman. Competent handbooks on *Broadcast English* contain recommendations to announcers based upon 'information slowly gathered in Broadcasting House over a period of years'. Nevertheless, no special authority is claimed for the pronunciations recommended. They are 'but tentative solutions drawn up for the guidance of announcers'.

Over a period of thirty-four years (1913–47) the Society

for Pure English exercised its salutary influence and no lover of our language can help regretting that its series of highly specialized and informative Tracts have now come to an end. Robert Bridges was also this Society's founder and moving spirit. It was his belief that much could be done to preserve the *purity* of English, in the fullest and best sense, not by 'foolish interference with living developments' but by 'agreeing upon a modest and practical scheme for informing popular taste on sound principles, for guiding educational authorities, and for introducing into practice certain slight modifications and advantageous changes'. Bridges was supported by Sir William Craigie, Henry Watson Fowler, George Stuart Gordon, Logan Pearsall Smith, among others, but as these original members passed away, popular enthusiasm waned. The Society died not from lack of funds but from dearth of scholarly material of the quality and scope envisaged by its founders earlier in the century.

Why, it may be asked, should linguistic societies be so reluctant to assume responsibility for the control of 'good usage'? It is because few people sincerely regard such control as either desirable or practicable. Only twice in our history, in 1664 and in 1712, have we English made any serious attempt to follow the example of the Italians and the French in founding a linguistic Academy. The first attempt, associated with the name of Dryden, failed because scientific interests prevailed. The second, supported by Swift, was frustrated by a turn in political events.

'I have endeavoured to write English', said Dryden in his Dedication to *The Rival Ladies*, 'as near as I could distinguish it from the Tongue of Pedants, and that of affected Travellours. Only I am sorry that (speaking so noble a language as we do) we have not a more certain measure of it, as they have in France, where they have an Academy erected for that purpose and endowed with large privileges by the present King.' The Royal Society was just two years old and now, in 1664,

it showed its active interest in language as an instrument of
scientific thought by adopting a resolution to the effect that
as 'there were persons of the Society whose genius was very
proper and inclined to improve the English tongue, particularly for philosophic purposes, it was voted that there should
be a committee for improving the English language; and that
they meet at Sir Peter Wyche's lodgings in Gray's Inn once or
twice a month, and give an account of their proceedings,
when called upon'. This committee consisted of twenty-two
persons and it numbered John Dryden, John Evelyn, Edmund
Waller, and Thomas Sprat, Bishop of Rochester, among its
members. It was the nearest approach, so far, to the foundation
of an authoritative Academy in England. Nevertheless, however strongly charged it may have been by the scientists, this
committee lacked drive and energy. Perhaps its terms of reference were too vague and ill defined. It met only three or four
times and it achieved nothing of importance. As the Royal
Society grew in strength, so the attention of its Fellows became more and more completely absorbed by scientific research. Meantime, however, the popular notion that the English language might somehow be fixed, remained fashionable.
The Age of Reason, *Éclaircissement* or *Aufklärung*, was dawn-
ing, with its glowing conception of 'order and truth and of
the whole universe governed by law'. At the turn of the century Addison, Swift, Pope, and their friends were busily dis-
cussing the compilation of a Standard English Dictionary.
Addison had thoughts of undertaking the work himself and
he marked passages in Tillotson for the purpose. Like so many
of his contemporaries, Addison had not yet abandoned the
idea of 'universal grammar' or, as he called it, the 'analogy of
languages'. There were, he pointed out (in Paper No. 135 of
The Spectator), ambiguous constructions in English 'which will
never be decided till we have something like an Academy,
that by the best Authorities and Rules drawn from the Analogy of Languages shall settle all Controversies between

Grammar and Idiom'. A few months after the appearance of this paper, Swift addressed his letter to the Earl of Oxford, Lord Treasurer, which was published under the title *A Proposal for Correcting, Improving, and Ascertaining* (that is, making certain, fixing) *the English Tongue*. 'I do here', he wrote, 'in the name of all the learned and polite (cultured, well-bred) persons of the nation complain to your Lordship as first minister, that our language is extremely imperfect; that its daily improvements are by no means in proportion to its daily corruptions; that the pretenders to polish and refine it have chiefly multiplied abuses and absurdities; and that in many instances it offends against every part of grammar.' Swift's proposal was completely in accord with prevailing temperament and it was well received. But it was not destined to bear fruit. Queen Anne died in 1714. The Earl of Oxford and his fellow Tories, including Swift himself, lost all power. The *Proposal* became an historical document. As Voltaire shrewdly observed (in the twenty-fourth of his *Lettres Philosophiques*) the failure to achieve any sort of English Academy was partly political. No further attempt was made. The need of a dictionary was supplied by Samuel Johnson in 1755, and a few years later Joseph Priestley and Robert Lowth wrote their *Grammars*. As the century wore on, scepticism concerning the desirability of 'embalming a language' increased. Johnson was compelled to admit that he had 'flattered himself for a while' with the prospect of 'fixing our language', but that thereby 'he had indulged expectation which neither reason nor experience could justify'. Johnson's views were sound and his influence was paramount. The establishment of an Academy would mean both gain and loss. All in all, the loss would be greater than the gain. Meantime man's linguistic horizon was rapidly widening. Before the end of the century, in 1796, Sir William Jones had published his memorable words on the affinities of the Indo-European languages, and not long after that, Bopp, Rask, Grimm, and Pott were giving their great books on comparative philology to the world. The linguistic climate was changing. Correctness was felt to be a relative term. In any case, correctness was not to be prescribed by any sort of committee: it was to be measured by the standards of good use, or of the best use of the best writers.

The grammar books by Priestley and Lowth were succeeded by many others, the most notable of which was Lindley Murray's *English Grammar* of 1795. Like that finer linguistic critic of a later generation, Logan Pearsall Smith (1865-1946), Murray was born in America but he made his home in England. His grammar book held the field until the appearance of Alexander Bain's *Higher English Grammar* of 1863 with its supplementary *Manual of English Composition and Rhetoric* of 1866. Numerous other grammars were compiled, both descriptive (stating what people really *do* say), prescriptive (stating what people *should* say), and even *proscriptive* (stating what people *should not* say). Some of them were still entangled with threads from Ælius Donatus and Priscian, clinging tenaciously to the conviction that grammar meant primarily Latin grammar, and that somehow Latin grammar embodied universally valid canons of logic. All was changed with *A New English Grammar, Logical and Historical*, which appeared in two volumes in 1892 and 1898, by the greatest of all English philologists, Henry Sweet. The first and larger volume on Phonology and Accidence was an excellent guide to sounds and forms and the second small volume on Syntax was a masterpiece of its kind. 'Language is partly rational', wrote Sweet, 'partly irrational and arbitrary'. Apart from Sweet's works, no comprehensive English Grammars have been produced in England. In America excellent Grammars have been written by Krapp, Kennedy, and Curme; and in Germany by Mätzner, Krüger, Koch, Wendt, and many others. But by far the most elaborate presentations of English Grammar have been made by three Dutchmen, H. Poutsma, Etsko Kruisinga, and R W. Zandvoort; and by the Dane, Otto Jespersen. Because

English is an analytic language, syntax or sentence-structure is of paramount importance. Poutsma and Kruisinga were followers of Sweet who stressed the value and importance of independent observation. They therefore endeavoured to divest themselves of all those preconceived notions which had their ultimate source in the Greek grammar of Dionysius Thrax and which had hampered traditional grammarians ever since. To a large extent Poutsma and Kruisinga invented their special terminologies. Their own language was closely enough related to ours to enable them to feel and know English perfectly; at the same time, it was sufficiently different from ours to enable them to examine the complicated structure and organism of English from the outside and to discern subtleties and peculiarities which had eluded native observers. In his masterly *Handbook of English Grammar* for Dutch university students, which first appeared in 1945, and in an enlarged revised edition in 1948, Zandvoort made a close comparison between English and Dutch showing to what extent these two kindred tongues ran side by side in their clause-structures and sentence-patterns and where and how far they parted company. Otto Jespersen published the first part of his *Modern English Grammar on Historical Principles* in 1909 and he was still working on the sixth and seventh parts in 1943, when he died in his eighty-third year at Lundehave, his pleasant home overlooking the Sound near Elsinore. Three of his former pupils in the University of Copenhagen later completed these two final volumes, the seventh and last appearing in 1949. The first volume is devoted to sounds and spelling and the sixth to morphology or accidence, but all the other five are given over to syntax. Jespersen's great work is thus primarily a descriptive syntax of living English with an historical outlook. His more concise version in one volume, *The Essentials of English Grammar* (1933), is probably the favourite Grammar in daily use in England. Jespersen professed to represent English Grammar 'not as a set of stiff dogmatic precepts according to which some things are correct and others absolutely wrong, but as something living and developing under continual fluctuations and undulations, something that is founded on the past and prepares the way for the future, something that is not always consistent or perfect, but progressing and perfectible – in one word, human'. In his later years this famous Scandinavian Anglicist was highly honoured by scholars on both sides of the Atlantic, and yet he disclaimed 'any right to tell British and American readers what is correct or pure English, but only to register and, if possible, to explain the actual facts of English usage in various periods'. It was his impression that 'it would be a good thing if what might be called a Grammar of Relativity could be everywhere substituted for the Grammar of Rigidity taught in most schools all over the world'. Jespersen believed in 'progress in language' and he regarded English as a language in a very advanced stage. But what is progress in language? Because Jespersen was unduly optimistic, he was sometimes uncritical: yet he always wrote with such liveliness and zest that to read him is a tonic. Future grammarians will never cease to peruse his pages with profit and delight.

Jespersen's seven-volume Grammar contains a wealth of illustrative quotations after the pattern of *The New English Dictionary on Historical Principles*, now generally called *The Oxford English Dictionary*, which appeared in instalments over a period of forty-five years from 1883 to 1928. Its first editor, Sir James Murray, was responsible for over seven thousand of its pages, or nearly one half of the entire work. He was later assisted by three joint-editors, Henry Bradley, Sir William Craigie and Charles Talbut Onions, as well as by numerous contributors, sub-editors and assistants. The Dictionary fills twelve volumes, occupies over fifteen thousand pages, and contains 414,825 words illustrated by 1,827,306 citations. It is the Dictionary of the British Commonwealth and of the United States, a fact symbolized by the presentation of the first copies, in April, 1928, to King George V and President

Calvin Coolidge as the heads of the two English-speaking peoples. It aims at exhibiting the history and signification of words now in use or known to have been in use since the middle of the twelfth century. From A.D. 1150 to 1500 all the five dialects – Northern, East Midland, West Midland, Southern, and Kentish – were of equal literary importance and status and they are therefore all included. After 1500, however, British and American dialectal expressions are not admitted except in so far as they may have acquired a certain literary currency. If a word has been in use at any time after 1150, then its history is carried back to the earliest recorded form. Thus the greater part of the Old English vocabulary is included, but not all. So, for example, *ēðel* 'ethel, native land', *lēod* 'lede, people', and *þēod* 'thede, nation', appear in the Dictionary because they remained in use after the twelfth century; but *eoh* 'horse' (related to Latin *equus* and English *equine* and *equestrian*, and also to Greek *hippos* in *hippopotamus* 'river horse' and *Philip* 'lover of horses') does not appear for the simple reason that it was no longer a living word in Middle English. Otherwise the vocabulary is comprehensive and it even includes denizens (*aide-de-camp*, *locus*, *carte-de-visite*, and *table d'hôte*), aliens (*shah*, *geyser*, *cicerone*, *targum*, *backsheesh*, and *sepoy*) and casuals (expressions like Italian *podestà* 'magistrate' and *sbirro* 'police constable', found in books of foreign travel). Technical terms are included if they are used more widely outside their special fields. Because so many of the names of the peculiar technicalities of trades and processes are international and because they may vary from year to year, the twentieth-century lexicographer has to decide quite arbitrarily whether to admit or to reject them. They present him with problems unknown to Dr Johnson in the eighteenth century.

In exhibiting the signification of words that sense is placed first which was actually the earliest in time. The others follow in the order in which they appear to have arisen. Each separate sense is illustrated by quotations: the earliest recorded instance of a form is always given. These quotations are arranged chronologically so as to give at least one for each century. They are not annotated but they are left to speak for themselves. Exact references to books and editions are given so that the reader, if he so desires, may study each passage in its exact context. No other language in the world possesses such a complete guide as this. The First Supplement appeared in 1933 and in that year, too, a corrected re-issue was published under the title *The Oxford English Dictionary*. Its Transatlantic supplement in four volumes, *The Dictionary of American English on Historical Principles*, was completed by Sir William Craigie and James R. Hulbert in 1944. Corrections and additions are supplied from time to time by *The Bulletin of Historical Research*, *Transactions of the American Philological Association*, and other specialized journals. The influence of the Dictionary is not easily to be measured. Not only has it affected our whole attitude to language but it has raised the standard of all the numerous smaller dictionaries 'for school and home use' which adorn our bookstalls. It has made *The Shorter Oxford Dictionary* possible, as well as the matchless *Concise Oxford Dictionary of Current English* and *The Little Oxford Dictionary*. It has been used by the revisers of the great American encyclopaedic dictionaries, especially the *New Webster* and Funk and Wagnalls's *New Standard*. Only with its help was Henry Cecil Wyld able to compile his highly competent *Universal Dictionary*.

All the world looks to *The Oxford Dictionary* as the highest authority on all aspects of our language, but in matters of pronunciation foreigners rely more and more upon Professor Daniel Jones's *An English Pronouncing Dictionary*, the ninth edition of which, containing 56,280 words in International Phonetic Transcription, appeared in 1948. It is the author's expressed aim not to become 'either a reformer of pronunciation or a judge', but rather 'to observe and record accurately'. His book professes to record the sounds of 'typical Southern

English people in ordinary conversation' and that record is one 'of facts, not of theories or personal preferences'. It is a record of a form of speech that is both intelligible and pleasing to the greatest number of educated people throughout the English-speaking world. Sometimes Jones finds it imperative to give two acceptable pronunciations in order of frequency. The word *calibre*, for instance, may be stressed on the first syllable or on the second. In its transferred sense of 'weight of character, capacity of mind', it has become very fashionable: it has, in fact, become a *vogue-word*. Whatever its ultimate origin may be – it probably goes back to Arabic *qālib* 'mould, model' – the word has entered English by way of French *calibre*, which is disyllabic and, like most French words, has the stress on the final syllable. Those persons, therefore, who insist on [kəˈliːbə] as the superior pronunciation, are really deciding in favour of an inherited French stress as against that natural anglicizing to [ˈkælɪbə] which took place hundreds of years ago in such forms as *'manner*, which was long pronounced *ma'nere*, or in a host of others like *city, nature, virtue, justice, honour*, and *sentence*. Jones's *Pronouncing Dictionary* is invaluable for the gathered information it presents on the names of places and families. Keighley in the West Riding of Yorkshire is named [kiːθlɪ] by its inhabitants, but Keighley as a family-name may be pronounced either [kiːlɪ] or [kailɪ]. Am I pedantic when I say [ʃrouzbərɪ] for Shrewsbury? Jones records this, but he puts the 'eye pronunciation' [ʃruːzbərɪ] first. A succinct and highly informative note follows: 'ʃrou- is the pronunciation used by those connected with Shrewsbury School and by many residents in the neighbourhood, especially members of county families. The form [ʃruː-] is used by outsiders, and is the common pronunciation heard in the town.' How, I wonder, will this note be worded in twenty-five years' time? Already foreign students of English are diligently comparing the most recent edition of the Dictionary with the first edition of 1917.

The conception of custom and common usage as the final measure of linguistic correctness found full, but somewhat individualistic, expression in Henry Watson Fowler's *A Dictionary of Modern English Usage* (1926, corrected editions 1930 and 1937), which is now a standard work of reference and which holds a position of authority which its own editor would have been the first to disclaim. Many would agree with Professor Kemp Malone of Baltimore (in *Modern Language Notes*, 1927) that the book 'gives us the conclusions of a learned and charming dilettante rather than those of a man of science. It is a collection of linguistic prejudices persuasively presented by a clever advocate; it is not an objective, scientific presentation of the facts of English usage.' None the less, however, it has since won acceptance as a first-class authority and its weighty influence is apparent in the popular handbooks of more recent writers on various aspects of current speech: Robert Graves, Eric Partridge, Sir Alan Herbert, and Sir Ernest Gowers. All that these able writers have said on language has been challenging, provocative, and generally helpful. The popularity of their books testifies to an ever-growing awareness of the power of words. Nevertheless, the incessant interplay between tradition and experiment still presents a contradictory picture. However persistently they may proclaim that they record the details of everyday usage and that they merely state how men do speak and not how men ought to speak, the fact remains that twentieth-century lexicographers, grammarians, and phoneticians are becoming the arbiters of good speech in spite of themselves. Usage is hailed as the criterion in theory. In practice the reputable handbook is accepted as the authority more than ever before.

CHAPTER XI

Slang and Dialect

WE naturally tend to think of speech levels in terms of good, better, and best, and we incline to regard the transition from high rhetoric to low slang as a descent in the scale of values. A lively speaker should be able to express himself at various levels to suit the occasion. Swift deplored the use of slang by learned divines in their preaching, and Gibbon was conscious of the dignity of history when he spoke in his *Autobiography* of 'the proper tone, the peculiar mode of historical eloquence'. Even Gibbon would probably have allowed the historian to 'have his little joke' and to have occasional recourse to colloquial and slang phrases in order to relieve the monotony of a difficult expository lecture, but would he have approved of slang in the lecturer's published text-book? Text-books should be as sparkling and as vivacious as may be, but not too chatty and trivial in style: they should be able to stand up well to a second or a third reading. Language is like dress. We vary our dress to suit the occasion. We do not appear at a friend's silver wedding anniversary in gardening clothes nor do we go punting on the river in a dinner-jacket. Slang is like light music. The unprejudiced music-lover enjoys light music in its proper setting. We shall find plenty of slang in Chaucer, Shakespeare, and Ben Jonson. Whether we think of poetry as 'a remoter way of thinking' (Davenant), or 'the best words in the best order' (Coleridge), or 'the rhythmic creation of the beautiful' (Poe), we have to recognize that it has been written at all levels ranging from the liturgical solemnity and majesty of

Milton's *Hail holy light* as the exordium of Book III of *Paradise Lost* to the unconventional verses of *The Ingoldsby Legends* or the Indian Army slang of Kipling's *Gunga Din*.

Colloquial speech, as the epithet implies, is that of spoken conversation, easy without being slovenly, conventional but not formal. Good conversation lies behind much of the best literature in the world, and it has flourished more profusely at some periods than at others: in the Athens of Pericles, the Rome of the Antonines, the Florence of Dante, the Paris of Louis Quatorze, and the London of Dr Johnson. To-day we are all in too much of a hurry. Too seldom 'we cross our legs and have our talk out'. Even our letters are rarely expansive. Jane Austen's heroines thought nothing of devoting a long summer's day to the writing of one unimportant epistle. In letters, as well as in diaries and autobiographies, we find recorded the colloquial language of bygone ages. In our own letters we fail to communicate our feelings if we 'speak like a book'. The secret of successful letter-writing is simplicity itself. Imagine that the person you are addressing is sitting on the other side of the table and write down just what you have to say straightforwardly, easily, and without effort or affectation. Human sympathy and understanding are so very much more important in letter-writing than linguistic precision. Many a popular broadcaster owes his success to a simple exercise of the imagination. He may have nothing of the personality of a Sir Walford Davies, but all is well with him. Behind the microphone, within the studio itself, he sees with the 'inward eye' an appreciative and sympathetic group of friends. They are all there quietly listening, and while to them he reads his duly edited and censored typescript, his voice assumes colloquial tones, rhythms, cadences, and pauses, spontaneously and unobtrusively. The Reith Lecturer may adopt a different technique. His imaginary audience is listening in a cosy university aula: sensitive, attentive, more critical, but likewise friendly. The lecture must obviously be pitched at correspondingly higher speech levels, ranging from the literary to the common with only an occasional colloquial undertone.

As long ago as 1785 Francis Grose compiled *A Classical Dictionary of the Vulgar Tongue*, the first large serious collection of slang expressions. It was not by chance that this book was published on the eve of the French Revolution when men's interest in the ways and words of the lower classes was awakening. Our present attitude towards slang is more scientific than in Grose's day. We now regard slang as a series or group of speech forms which has its own right to exist and which is the most productive of all the sources of new expressions. Slang is worthy of study in any language. It may be ephemeral, living on the lips of men for a day, for a year, or for a decade – no more. Is there anything more dead than last year's slang? Some slang terms – *to booze*, for instance (Middle English *bousen* from Middle Dutch) 'to drink to excess', or *to rook* (Elizabethan English from the substantive *rook* in the sense of 'card-sharper') 'to cheat, swindle, charge exorbitantly' – may hover on the outskirts of respectability not only for years but even for centuries, and neither go out of use entirely nor yet gain admittance to the standard vocabulary. Others may go up in the world. Swift once deplored (in *The Tatler*, No. 230) the use of *I'd, can't, he's, shan't*, which he termed 'abbreviations and elisions, by which consonants of most obdurate sound are joined together, without one softening vowel to intervene'; and he inveighed against that 'refinement which consists in pronouncing the first syllable in a word that has many, and dismissing the rest, such as *phizz, hipps, mobb, pozz, rep*, and many more, when we are already overloaded with monosyllables, which are the disgrace of our language'. Now *hipps, pozz*, and *rep* are heard no more, but *phiz* still lives and has, perhaps, risen a little. It is described by *The Oxford English Dictionary* as 'humorous colloquial'. *Mob*, from Latin *mobile* (older *movibile*) *vulgus* 'the movable or excitable crowd', has risen yet higher. In Australian English it denotes a crowd without any disparaging implication.

There is good slang and bad slang. Good slang, in the words of G. K. Chesterton, is 'the one stream of poetry which is constantly flowing. ... Every day some nameless poet weaves some fairy tracery of popular language. ... The world of slang is a kind of topsy-turvydom of poetry, full of blue moons and white elephants, of men losing their heads, and men whose tongues run away with them – a whole chaos of fairy tales'. Good slang 'hits the nail on the head'. Bad slang 'misses the mark'. Bad slang is less effective than normal speech because it conveys only a vague and doubtful meaning. Catch-phrases may be bad slang, the lazy man's worn-out tunes, the much-soiled counters of intellectual and linguistic bankruptcy. Slogans may be bad slang, especially those vote-catching half-truths which are framed to play upon the emotions of an undiscerning section of the community.

Why should people not be content to 'call a spade a spade'? Their motives for using slang can seldom be analysed convincingly, but in general they seek three things in various degrees and proportions: novelty, vivacity, and intimacy. Slang proceeds from a new way of looking at things and it exercises every form of intellectual wit and verbal ingenuity. Slang is picturesque, livens up a dull theme and administers salutary jolts or shocks to listeners. Slang increases intimacy because it allows the speaker to drop into a lower key, to meet his fellow on even terms and to have 'a word in his ear'. Queen Victoria resented being addressed by Gladstone in private 'as if he were addressing a public meeting'. Now, because slang is intimate, it passes imperceptibly into secret or cryptic language and that is why the boundaries between slang and cant are hard to discern and define. Public school slang is a form of cant. It is an inherited esoteric lingo changing from school to school, from Westminster to Winchester and from Rugby to Shrewsbury. Gownsmen's slang is meant to be unintelligible to townsmen and it varies from university to university, from Oxford to Cambridge and from Liverpool

to Leeds. Again, because slang is intimate, it is sometimes con-
fined to a particular geographical community and thus ac-
quires features which are local and regional. That is why the
boundaries between slang and dialect are often uncertain and
vague. Slang and dialect meet and mingle in London Cockney,
that racy, spontaneous, picturesque, witty, and friendly English spoken not only by Londoners 'born within the sound of
Bow Bells' (the bells of St Mary-le-Bow Church in Cheap-
side) but also by millions of other Londoners living within a
forty-mile radius of the 'mother of cities'. As a dialect, London Cockney is both regional and social. Moreover, manual
workers, dockers, postmen, retail tradesmen, house decorators,
commercial travellers, printers, publishers, journalists, law-
yers, medical practitioners, politicians, artists, actors, sports-
men, and members of many other professions and callings
have their own ever-changing varieties of slang.

Students of language have detected a striking similarity
between the slang of the ancient world and that of to-day.
The comedies of Aristophanes and Menander, of Plautus and
Terence are re-interpreted and revitalized in the light of present-day slang. From Vulgar Latin and from Roman army
slang the great Romance languages – French, Spanish, Portuguese, Italian, and Romanian – have largely derived. There is
no doubt, for example, that the words for 'head' and 'leg' in
French and Italian derive from Latin slang and not from the
standard or literary language. The word for 'head' in classical
Latin was *caput*, genitive *capitis* (whence our *capital* and *chapter*),
but *testa* 'an earthen pot' has ousted *caput* in both French (*la
tête*) and Italian (*la testa*): it must once have been as slangy as
Shakespearian *costard* 'apple', *mazard* 'bowl', and *sconce* 'lantern',
or modern *napper*, *onion*, *rocker*, and *block*. The word for 'leg'
was *crus*, genitive *cruris* (as in *crural* artery), but *crus* gave place
to *gamba* 'hoof' (French *la jambe*, Italian *la gamba*), which must
have been as slangy as modern *stumps* and *pins*. *Salary* was
'salt-money', a Roman soldier's allowance for the purchase of

salt, and hence, cynically, his pay. A man who 'heels' or kicks back is *recalcitrant* (Latin *calcitrāre* 'to kick' from *calx, calcis* 'heel'): when he 'jumps on' his foe he *assails* him (Latin *ad* 'to' + *salīre* 'to jump'), or *assaults* him (Latin *ad* + *saltus* 'jumping'), and when he 'keeps on jumping on' his foe he *insults* him (Latin *in* 'into' + *saltāre* or *sultāre* frequentative 'to keep on jumping'). Bogus seventeenth-century Latin has given us *hoax* from *hocus-pocus*, invented by a conjurer as 'a dark composure of words, to blind the eyes of the beholders, to make his trick pass the more currently without discovery'. Law Latin has given us *ignoramus* 'we do not know', that is, 'we take no notice of (it)', which was first applied in the seventeenth century to an ill-informed lawyer and now to any ignorant person.

Common sense is the internal sense or awareness which serves as a bond or common centre for the five external senses of sight, hearing, smell, taste, and touch. The Americans often speak of *horse sense*, which *The Century Dictionary* defines as 'a coarse, robust, and conspicuous form of shrewdness often found in ignorant and rude persons; plain, practical good sense'. It is akin to *mother wit* where *mother*, as in *mother country* and *mother tongue*, is a survival of the Old English *r*- stem genitive. In Negro and Pidgin English mother wit is *savvy* or *savey*, after the Spanish *sabe usted* 'you know'. *Gumption* is another close synonym, short for Northern and Scottish *rum-gumption* and *rumblegumption*, which are not older than the eighteenth century and are of highly controversial etymology.

A *beak* or a *beck* was a policeman before he became a magistrate or a schoolmaster. A nineteenth-century policeman was nicknamed a *peeler* or a *bobby*, for he came into being in 1828 when the Metropolitan Police Act was passed and when Sir Robert Peel was Home Secretary. He was also dubbed a *body-snatcher*. He is still referred to affectionately as a *bobby* (after Bobby Peel), a *man in blue*, an *arm of the law*, and a *copper*, one who *cops* or *caps* (Latin *capere* 'to take'). Have you ever thought of the numerous slang terms for 'money' which have been fashionable in your own experience? In his *Dictionary of Modern Slang, Cant and Vulgar Words* (1859) John Camden Hotten noted over one hundred slang expressions for 'the necessary', and scores of others have since 'had their day'. Think, too, of all the countless terms for *excellent* which you may have heard recently from your more exuberant friends: *kiff, posh, swell, ripping, grand, stunning, smashing, topping, topnotch, top-hole, A1, first-class, yum-yum, champion, fine, superfine, super, extra-super,* and *super-super*. There seem to be so many phases and forms of *nonsense* rampant under the sun that the procession of slang synonyms grows ever longer and longer: *balderdash, ballyhoo* (from *bally hooly*), *bilge* ('foul water in the bottom of a ship's hull'), *blab, blague, blah, blather* (Old Norse *blaðr*) with its collaterals *blether, blither,* and *blother; bosh* (a Turkish word made current by its frequent appearance in J. J. Morier's novel *Ayesha,* 1834, which achieved great popularity in the 'Standard Novels' edition); *buncombe, bunkum,* or *bunk* (from Buncombe, a county in North Carolina, whose member in the sixteenth Congress insisted on making a fatuous speech when the debate on the Missouri Question was nearing its close, just because 'the people of his district expected it of him'), *claptrap, drivel, flapdoodle, fudge, gammon* (or *gammon and patter*), *guff, gup* (or *gup gup*), *hooey, hot air, humbug, mush, piffle, pop* (short for *poppycock*), *pulp, rot* (or *tommy rot*), *rubbish, slaver, slush, stuff* (or *stuff and nonsense*), *tosh, trash, tripe,* and *twaddle*. Think of all the expressions you have ever heard for 'Be off! Depart!': *Beat it, buzz off, clear off* or *out, decamp, disappear, evaporate* (common in the eighteenth century and in Dickens), *fade away, get along with you, get out, get you gone* (where *you* is reflexive, like thee in Shakespeare's 'Go, get thee gon, fetch me an iron Crow': *Comedy of Errors,* III. i. 84), *go away, go to Bath* (*blazes, China, Jericho, Timbuctoo,* and countless other places), *hop it, imshi* (Army slang from Arabic in the First World War), *make off, push off, quit, scram, shog off* ('Will you shogge off?' Shakespeare's *Henry the Fifth*, II. i. 47), *shoo* (*shooshoo, shoo shoo*, an instinctive exclamation used in some such form in many languages to drive away birds), *shove off* (as in a boat, *shove* itself being a dignified verb from Old English), *skedaddle* (probably a fanciful formation), *skiddoo* (a Canadian variant of *skedaddle*), *sling your hook* (that is, your miner's *hooked bag*, containing belongings not required down the shaft), *turf off* (*to turf it* is 'to take to the turf, to be on the tramp' in American slang), *twenty-three*, *vamoose* (Mexican from Spanish *vamos* 'let us go'), and many more.

As we have seen, Swift disapproved of such *clippings* or stump-words as *mob* and *cab*, but Johnson had no such linguistic scruples, for, as we learn from Boswell's *Life*, he even 'had a way of contracting the names of his friends, as Beauclerc, *Beau*; Boswell, *Bozzy*; Langton, *Lanky*; Murphy, *Mur*; Sheridan, *Sherry*; and Goldsmith, *Goldy*, which Goldsmith resented'. Such clippings are rife in slang, whether by *aphesis*, omission of initial unstressed syllables, or by *apocope*, suppression of end sounds. *Van* may come from *caravan* by aphesis or from *vanguard* by apocope. *Caravan* comes from Persian *karwan*, which found its way into Old French at the time of the Crusades and into the Anglo-Latin of Roger of Hoveden and Matthew Paris, but which did not appear in English until 1599 in Richard Hakluyt's *Voyages*. *Vanguard* derives from the French *avantgarde* by the operation of aphesis long ago in the fifteenth century. In daily conversation we are seldom conscious in the act of speaking that we are indulging in abbreviations, that *on tick* is short for 'on ticket'; (Government party) *whip* for *whipper-in*; *fag* for 'fag-end of a cigarette'; *tam* for 'tam-o'-shanter cap' from Tam (Tom) of Shanter, the hero of Burns's poem of that name; *snap* from 'snapshot picture or photograph'; and that *stock* really stands for 'stock gillyflower', which has a stronger stock or stem than the clove gillyflower or pink. Historically a *wag* is a 'waghalter', a man likely to wag a halter or swing at the end of a rope, a man fit to be hanged. The sense of 'witty fellow' is more recent. A *quack* is a 'quacksalver', a man who quacks, puffs or boasts about his salves or secret remedies. A *coster* is a 'costermonger', a seller in the London streets of *costards*, or large, prominently ribbed apples (Old French *coste*, Modern French *côte* 'rib'). A *cat*, in 'no room to swing a cat', is a 'cat-o'-nine tails', a whip with nine knotted lashes. A *coon* is a *bloke* (of unknown origin), a *chap* (chapman, merchant), a *cove* (Gypsy), a *guy* (after Guy Fawkes), or a *wallah* (Hindustani). *Coon* is shortened by aphesis from *racoon*, the North American Indian name for the Old Whig party of the United States, which at one time had the racoon as its emblem. A *rickshaw* is a 'man-power-carriage', Japanese *jin-riki-shaw*.

Inasmuch as they are cryptic languages, Cockney rhyming slang, back slang, and centre slang lie over the borderline separating slang from cant. *To half-inch*, in the sense 'to steal, purloin', is thieves' cant. We look for *half-inch* in the dictionaries and we do not find it, although it is an expression heard all over England. It is genuine rhyming slang for *pinch*, which is first recorded in this sense in Richard Head's *The canting academy, or, the devil's cabinet, opened with several new catches and songs* of 1673. So 'wife' becomes *trouble and strife*, and 'money' *bees and honey*. 'Table' might be a thousand things, but in this particular lingo it is *Cain-and-Abel* and nothing else. 'Stairs' are *apples and pears*, 'boots' *daisy-roots*, 'eyes' *mince-pies*, and 'feet' *plates of meat*. Still more ingenious terms may be devised when the rhyming word is suppressed and 'hat' becomes *tit-for* (-tat), 'heart' *raspberry* (tart), 'fist' *Oliver* (Twist), and 'mouth' *north* (and south). The self-appointed creators of back slang do not hesitate to take certain liberties in the interests of euphony and pronounceability. 'Game' is simply *emag* and 'market' *tekram*, but 'police' is *slop* and 'penny' is, with the insertion of anaptyctic *e*, *yennep*. Similarly 'pint' becomes *tenip*, 'girl' *elrig*, 'old maid' *delo diam*, 'old woman' *delo nammow* and 'drunk' *kennurd*. *Kacab genals* is back slang for 'back slang'.

In centre or medial slang a vowel and its following consonant constitute the first two sounds and the remainder of the word is framed somewhat capriciously. Thus 'cheek' becomes *eekcher*, 'mug' *ugmer*, 'fool' *oolfoo*, and 'proper' *operpro*. Varieties of Cockney slang and other lowly forms of speech rose from the underworld during the First and Second World Wars and spread far and wide among the men and women of the three fighting services, acquiring a new lease of life thereby.

The genuine regional dialects of Britain have tended to decline in recent years. School, radio, and film do not favour the preservation of local speech. Other factors conducive to the decline of regional dialect are snobbishness; the 'rush to the towns' and the subsequent urbanization of life; the uprooting of families as a result of 'total war'; and, by no means least, the general dearth of traditional dialect literature after the rise of standard English in the fifteenth century. It was unfortunate that the scientific study of dialects, or linguistic geography as it is now fashionable to call it, was not inaugurated in this country until many of the richest and most interesting forms of regional speech were already passing away. Lovers of the English language, and especially lovers of English medieval literature, will never cease to deplore this misfortune, because they know that, in the last resort, the key to the precise interpretation of a Middle English text may be found in the living dialectal expressions of a later time. From one point of view all medieval English literature was dialectal. As our language changes, as we move farther and farther away in time from the great nameless poets of the thirteenth century, from Chaucer and Langland in the fourteenth, from Richard Rolle and Walter Hilton, so their language calls for renewed exegesis. That is why it was something of a tragedy that *The English Dialect Society* began its work so late and that Alexander John Ellis's account of *The Present English Dialects*, which formed Part V of his voluminous work *On Early English Pronunciation*, did not appear until 1889.

Ellis divided England and Wales into *regions* and *districts*, numbering the districts from 1 to 42, ignoring the great cities. He depicted the first, second, and third districts as areas lying beyond the confines of England and Scotland and comprising respectively the old Elizabethan colony around Wexford in the extreme south-east of Ireland, and the Pembroke and the Gower peninsulas in South Wales. Thence he proceeded with his picture of the English and Scottish dialects lying east of C.B. or the Celtic Border from south to north, at last reaching the fortieth district at Wick in Caithness, the forty-first in the Orkneys, and the forty-second in the Shetlands. The two maps appended to Ellis's book are rough and crude according to present-day standards, but they are generally reliable. They are, in fact, unique. In spite of its manifest limitations and deficiencies Ellis's record has a permanent value.

Not many years later Joseph Wright began work on *The English Dialect Dictionary* (1896–1905), which included *The English Dialect Grammar* (1905), presenting 'the complete vocabulary of all dialect words still in use or known to have been in use during the last two hundred years'. Wright was acutely conscious of the urgency of his self-imposed task. Was he not at least a century too late? Therefore he and his wife, Elizabeth Mary Wright, laboured incessantly for many years to collect and preserve the treasured speech-forms of the villages, hamlets, and farmsteads of the English and Scottish countryside, speech-forms which were gradually being forgotten as older generations passed away. Wright's earlier study (1892) of the dialect of his own native village of Windhill in the West Riding, 'the only language he really knew', now stood him in good stead. It was among the first of a series of eclectic studies of well-defined regional dialects spoken by communities far removed from populous centres of industry and from main lines of communication. These studies were made by men who had better technical training than Ellis had possessed, in both phonetics and general linguistics. Above all, they were competent to record and interpret sounds accurately and unambiguously in international phonetic transcription. Their monographs differ widely in shape, scope, method, and achievement. Among the more important ones are the studies of the Pewsey dialect in Wiltshire by J. Kjederqvist, written in Swedish (1903), of West Somerset by Etsko Kruisinga, written in Dutch (1904), of Lorton in Cumberland by Börje Brilioth (1913), of Hackness in the North Riding by G. H. Cowling (1915), of Penrith by P. H. Reaney (1927), of Huddersfield by W. E. Haigh (1928), of Suffolk by Helge Kökeritz (1932), of Byers Green in South Durham by Harold Orton (1933), of Lindsey by J. E. Oxley (1940), and of Dorset by Bertil Widén (1949). These studies have been made by individuals fortuitously. The Philological Society has recently planned to undertake a co-ordinated survey of the living dialects of Great Britain which may eventually be incorporated into a *Linguistic Atlas* comparable with those already produced by Jules Gilliéron and E. Edmont for France (1902–10), by Karl Jaberg and Jakob Jud for Italy and Southern Switzerland (1928–40), and by Hans Kurath for New England (1939–43).

Four out of five of the people of England live in cities, but there is no reason why town-dwellers should turn a deaf ear to dialect or deliberately miss the point of so many wise old proverbs. A cold May and a windy makes a full barn and a *findy* (substantial). A man may *speer the gate* (ask the way) to Rome. Better *fleech* (flatter) a fool than fight him. Cross the stream where it is *ebbest* (shallowest). Eat leeks in *Lide* (March) and *ramsins* (ramson, garlic) in May and all the year after physicians may play. For a *tint* (lost) thing care not. He that *lippens* (trusts) to lent ploughs, his land will lie *ley* (unploughed, fallow). It is a good tree that hath neither *knap* (knob) nor *gaw* (blemish). Keep a calm *sough* (silence). *Mum* (silence) is counsel. Let every man be content with his own *kevel* (lot). Mickle *maun* (must) a good heart *thole* (endure).

CHAPTER XII

Names of Persons and Places

IF you open casually *The Dictionary of National Biography*, *The London Directory*, or any telephone directory, and read through a list of names, you are conscious at once that many names have some kind of meaning, that many are clearly names of places, and that many more are apparently not English at all, but Scottish perhaps, or Welsh, Irish, Dutch, Scandinavian, or merely exotic.

It is easy to understand that in the early stages of a language the first words are names, and that all names are primarily proper names. Generic names, like *man*, *animal*, and *tree*, evolve later; and abstractions, like *courage*, *ferocity*, and *greenness*, later still. A proper name is a symbol pointing to one and only one person, animal, place, or thing. Primitive man felt that the relationship between name and thing (between symbol and referend) was close and intimate. The frivolous or malicious handling of a name in speech might imply insult or injury to the person bearing that name. The very name was hallowed.

The Anglo-Saxons, like their Continental kinsmen, followed well-defined principles in naming their sons and daughters. In fact, they took their name-giving very seriously. Most names were dithematic, consisting of two elements or themes, like the modern *Alf-red*, *Cuth-bert*, *Dun-stan*, *Ed-mund*, *Her-bert*, and *Wini-fred*. These elements were interchanged, repeated, and varied among members of a family and they were chosen for the sake of alliteration in order that they might be handed down from generation to generation in the ancient patterns of alliterative verse. All Old English poetry was alliterative. The vowels alliterated together: in names vocalic alliteration was commonest. Over seventy known descendants of Ecgbeorht, King of Wessex, father of Æthelwulf and grandfather of Ælfred the Great, had names with initial vowels. The father's name might have one of its themes *varied* in that of the son and its two themes *repeated* in that of the grandson, in whom he devoutly anticipated that his courageous spirit, with his name, might live again when he himself had departed. Sometimes a child received one element of his name from his father and one from his mother. Thus the saintly prelate Wulfstan, the last pre-Norman Bishop of Worcester, derived the first part of his name from his mother Wulfgifu and the second theme from his father Æthelstan. Some of these Old English names look like translations from Greek, but the correspondence may be fortuitous. *God-wine* is Greek *Theó-philos*; *God-giefu* (Latinized as *Godiva*) is Greek-derived *Doro-thy* (or, with themes reversed, *Theo-dore*); and *Sigebeorht* (modern *Seabright*) is *Nico-phanes*.

The men and women of Anglo-Saxon England normally bore one name only. Distinguishing epithets were rarely added. These might be patronymic (*Ælfrēd Æðelwulfing* 'son of Æthelwulf'), descriptive (*Ēadweard sē langa* 'tall Edward'), titular (*Cynewulf prēost* 'priest') or occupational (*Ēadmund fugelere* 'fowler'). They were, however, hardly surnames. Heritable family names gradually became general in the three centuries or so immediately following the Norman Conquest. It was not until the thirteenth and fourteenth centuries and the two or three generations before Geoffrey Chaucer (Chaucier or Chaussier, Modern French *chausseur* 'shoemaker') that surnames became fixed, although, for many years after that, the degree of stability in family names varied considerably in different parts of the country. Even in Chaucer's day (*c.* 1340–1400) the font-name was still *the* name and in the course of his life a man might assume many non-font-names or, yet more likely, he might have them thrust upon him by his friends and acquaintances. Servants and apprentices and even mature journeymen might be known by the names of their masters. *Richards* may mean 'Richard's man' as well as 'Richard's son'.

After the Norman Conquest Biblical names became fashionable, and of these *Mary* and *John* were easily first. The figures of those eyewitnesses of the Crucifixion, the mother of Christ and the 'beloved disciple', were seen by all men beneath the chancel arches of the parish churches of Europe. Even to-day *Mary* and *John* are by far the commonest Christian names in the west, rivalled only by *Ann(e)*, *Elizabeth*, *David*, *Michael*, and *Peter*. *John*, indeed, 'God is gracious', assumes many euphonious forms: Gaelic *Ian* or *Iain*, Irish *Sean*, *Shane*, or *Shawn*, Welsh *Evan*, German *Hans*, French *Jean*, Spanish *Juan*, Italian *Giovanni*, Greek *Zan* or *Zanet*, Czech *Jan*, and Russian *Ivan*. Let us imagine that a tall young Englishman named John is living in the thirteenth century in a pleasant Merseyside village near to which I happen to be writing these lines. John lives by the green in the village of Hale in the County Palatine of Lancaster. He earns his livelihood mainly by making wains or wagons for neighbouring farms. His father's name is Peter. He himself is plain John and he inclines to resent being called by any other name. But there are several other Johns in the neighbourhood from whom our John must somehow be distinguished in daily conversation although, when he delivers his well-made haywains at outlying farms, he is sometimes greeted as John Peterson of Hale. He is, to be sure, *John Peterson Long at Hale Green Wainwright*, and as long as he lives, he may be known by any single one or by any combination of these five occasional surnames. His present-day descendants may bear numerous possible names. If John's own children were named after him, they and their descendants might be known as *John*, *Johns*, *Johnson*, *Jones*,

Jone, Jack, Jacks, Jackson, Jake, Jenkin (from the English diminutive or hypocoristic form 'dear little Johnnie'), *Jenkins, Jenkinson, Jenning* (from the French diminutive *Jeanin*), *Jennings, Jennison, Hankin, Hankins, Hankinson,* or *Hancock.* If, however, John's father's name clung yet more closely, so that his own children were named after their grandfather in this critical period when surnames were becoming stable, then they and their descendants might be called *Peter, Peters, Peterson, Piers, Pierce, Peers, Pearson, Perrin, Perkin, Parkin, Perkins, Parkins, Perkinson,* or *Parkinson.* John's tallness might be commemorated in *Long, Lang,* or *Laing*; or his dwelling by the village-centre in *Green*; or the name of the village in *Hale* or *Hales*; or his chosen handicraft in *Wainwright, Wright* (from Old English), or *Smith* (from English or Scandinavian). All are likely possibilities. Cousins, when once they were separated, might bear diverse names or variants of the same family name.

It is certainly interesting to bear these facts in mind as we peruse lists of names in dictionary or directory. Before long we shall discover that British surnames fall mainly into four broad categories: patronymic, occupational, descriptive, and local. A few names, it is true, will remain puzzling: foreign names, perhaps, crudely translated, adapted or abbreviated; or artificial names. Over 50 per cent of genuine British surnames derive from place-names of various kinds and so they belong to the last of our four main categories. Even such a name as *Simpson* may belong to this last group and not to the first if the family once had its home in the ancient village of that name in Berkshire, the *Swinestone* of Domesday Book, Old English *Sigewines tūn* 'farmstead of Sigewine or victory-friend'. Otherwise *Simpson* means 'the son of Simon or Simeon', as might be expected, the Scandinavian *-son* (Danish *-sen*, Swedish *-son*) gradually supplanting the Old English patronymic *-ing* which we have already encountered in *Æthelwulfing*. The original Christian name may be unchanged, or little changed, as in the typically English names

Johnson and *Wilson*, or it may be modified, as in *Addison*, son
of Adam; *Anderson*, of Andrew; *Batson*, of Bartholomew;
Dawson, of David; *Grierson*, of Gregory; *Henderson*, of Henry;
Hobson, of Robert (from *Hob*, rhyming form of *Rob*); *Musson*,
of Erasmus; and *Olson*, of Olaf. The suffix *-son* may also have
been added to the hypocoristic or 'pet' form of the Christian
name as in *Atkinson*, son of dear little Adam; *Collinson*, of
Nicholas; *Dickinson*, of Richard; *Hodgkinson*, of Roger;
Hutchinson, of Hugh; and *Wilkinson*, of William. In Gaelic
the prefix is *Mac-*, and so we may associate *Macgregor* with
Greggs, *Griggs*, *Gregson*, and *Grierson*; *Macalister* with *Sander-
son*, son of Alexander; and *McTavish* with *Davidson* and *Dawson*. Other well-known Gaelic patronymics are *MacCulloch*,
son of a man nicknamed the boar; *Macdonald*, of the world-
ruler; *MacDougall*, *MacDugald*, and *MacDowell*, of the dark
stranger or Dane; *MacGowan*, of the smith; and *MacIntyre*, of
the carpenter. Welsh *Map-* is cognate with Gaelic *Mac-*, but
it is best known in its forms *Ap-*, *P-*, or *B-* as in *Ap Rhys*,
Rees, *Rice*, *Price*, and *Bryce*, son of the king or ruler. Anglo-
Norman *Fitz-* corresponds to French *fils* and is preserved in
Fitzgerald, *Fitzpatrick*, *Fitzroy*, *Fitzstephen*, and many more.

Hundreds of occupational surnames are at once familiar to
us or are at least recognizable after a little thought: *Archer*,
Baker or *Baxter*, *Bowman*, *Butcher*, *Butler*, *Carpenter*, *Carter*,
Carver, *Chamberlain*, *Chapman*, *Clark(e)*, *Cook*, *Draper*, *Dyer*,
Farmer, *Fish* and *Fisher* (Old English weak noun *fisca* side by
side with *fiscere*), *Falconer* and *Fa(u)lkner*, *Forster* 'forester',
Fowler, *Fuller* 'one who fulls or cleanses cloth', *Gard(i)ner*,
Harper, *Hawker*, *Hedger*, *Herdman* and *Shepherd*, *Hooper*
'maker of hoops for barrels and casks', *Hunt*, *Hunter* (Old
English *hunta* and *huntere*) and *Todhunter* (*tod* 'fox'), *Mason*,
Miller and *Milner*, *Parker* and *Parkman*, *Porter* 'doorkeeper' or
'bearer, carrier', *Potter*, *Reeve* and *Sherriff* 'shire-reeve',
Roper, *Salter* 'salt-maker', 'dancer', or 'player on the harp or
psaltery', *Skinner*, *Taylor*, *Turner* 'one who turns or fashions

articles of wood or metal on a lathe', *Waller* 'rough mason or wall-builder', *Weaver*, *Webb* and *Webster* (old English *wefere, *webba*, and female *webbestre*). Hundreds of others are more obscure in their signification and testify to the amazing specialization in medieval arts, crafts, and functions. Such are *Amner* 'almoner, keeper of the cupboard'; *Badger* 'hawker, huckster'; *Bannister* (Old French *balestier*) 'cross-bow man'; *Barker* 'tanner'; *Bateman* 'boatman'; *Biller* 'maker of axes or bills'; *Band* or *Bond* (Old Norse *bónda*) 'farmer, householder', whence also *Husband* and *Younghusband*; *Bolter* 'sifter of meal'; *Curtler* 'maker of kirtles or short gowns'; *Day* (Old English *dæge*, gradational variant of *-dige* in *hlæfdige* 'lady', literally 'loaf-kneader') 'maker or kneader of bread', later 'dairymaid', and later still 'male farm-hand', whence also *Faraday*, *Fereday* and *Ferriday* 'itinerant farm labourer'; *Fletcher*, *Flecker*, and *Flicker* 'maker of bows and arrows'; *Fuster* 'saddle-tree-maker'; *Gaiter* (Old French *gaitier*) 'watchman'; *Horner* 'maker of horn spoons and combs'; *Keeler* 'bargeman'; *Latimer* (Old French *latimier* for *latinier*) 'Latiner, interpreter'; *Latter* 'lath-maker'; *Lorimer* 'maker of straps (Latin *lōrum* 'thong') and metal mountings for horses' bridles'; *Mather* 'mower' (Modern English *aftermath* 'after-mowing'); *Panter* 'officer of a household who supplied the bread (Latin *pānis*) and had charge of the pantry'; *Pilcher* 'maker of pilches or coarse woollen garments'; *Pitcher* 'one who covers or caulks with pitch'; *Pounder*, *Pinder*, and *Poinder* 'one whose office it is to pound cattle'; *Ripper* 'reaper'; *Shermer*, *Shurmer*, *Skirmer* and *Skurmer* 'fencer, swordsman'; *Souter* 'cobbler'; *Spencer* and *Spenser* 'dispenser, steward of a household'; *Spooner* 'one who covers a roof with shingles'; *Tasker* 'one who threshes corn with a flail as task-work or piece-work'; *Tozer* 'teaser of cloth'; *Walker* 'fuller of cloth'; and *Warner* for *Warrener* 'game-keeper in a park or preserve'. One and the same man might play many parts, within doors and without, according to the season of the year. He might be hedger, reaper, harper, and bowman, and to him and to his children after him any one of these four occupational surnames might then cling. Furthermore, he might love to exercise his histrionic gifts when a pageant was staged in the neighbouring town and he might there play his part with such outstanding competence that his friends would never forget his brilliant acting all their days. Even his regular vocations would then recede in significance and the name *Pope*, *Cardinal*, *Bishop*, or *Leggatt* (Legate) might stick to him and his – or *Caesar*, perhaps, *King*, *Prince*, or *Duke*.

All these vocational and avocational names carry with them a certain gravity and dignity which descriptive names often lack. Some, it is true, like *Long* and *Lang*, *Strong* and *Strang*, *Short* and *Little*, *Broad* and *Large*, are simple. They may be taken quite literally. Others require more circumspection: their meanings are slightly different from the modern ones. *Black* and *White* implied 'dark, brunette' and 'fair, blond' respectively. *Sharp* meant genuinely 'discerning, alert, acute' rather than 'quick-witted, clever', and its antonym *Blunt* signified 'insensitive, dull, obtuse' rather than 'plain-spoken, abrupt'. *Moody* meant both 'courageous, high-spirited' and 'stubborn, wilful', but it did not acquire its present meaning until Shakespeare's time. In the name-giving centuries *Stout* was a highly laudatory appellation denoting 'valiant, brave, resolute'. It did not come to mean 'fat, corpulent' until the nineteenth century.

What could be more natural than that men should be known by some physical or external characteristic? *Head* and *Foot*, *Fist* (German *Faust*, French *Poincaré* for *poing carré* 'square fist'), *Thumb*, *Tooth* (French *Dent*) or *Lock* (of hair) might become surnames without any distinguishing epithet. More often, naturally, a qualifying adjective was added: *Broadhead*, *Fairhead* 'handsome', *Whitehead* 'fair', *Weatherhead* 'shaped like that of a wether or sheep'. The ending *-head* was often reduced to *-ett* as in *Blackett*, the opposite of *Whitehead*,

Brockett 'badger-head' and *Doggett* 'dog-head'. *Harlock* 'hoar or grey lock of hair' had its variant *Horlick*. *Harefoot* and *Lightfoot*, both 'fleet of foot', had their uncomplimentary antonym 'thick or stumpy foot' or *Puddifoot*. It was indeed remarkable that hard and insulting names should have clung to a man's children and to his children's children. Three famous Scottish names – *Cameron* 'crooked nose', *Campbell* 'crooked mouth', and *Kennedy* 'ugly head' – were hardly less disparaging. Men were frequently likened to animals and birds. In the eyes of the early Germanic peoples the bear and the boar were the kings of the forest, whereas the wolf and the raven were the close companions of the god Odin. These four creatures figured prominently in personal names throughout Western Europe for many centuries after the Heroic Age. *Bull* was a medieval name, but *John Bull*, that 'honest, plain-dealing fellow' whom with pride we regard as the typical Englishman, is not older than Dr John Arbuthnot's pamphlets in the age of Pope. A peculiarity of physiognomy or dress, a quality of mind or temperament, or even an eccentricity of conduct or behaviour might cause a man or woman to be dubbed *Calf*, *Cat*, *Colt*, *Doe*, *Hare*, *Hart*, *Hog*, *Roe*, *Squirrel*, or *Steer* by some shrewd neighbour. A man might be nicknamed *Fox* from his red hair or from his cunning ways. A vain fellow was called *Peacock* or *Pocock*. Other bird-names like *Crane*, *Crow*, *Daw*, *Dove*, *Eagle*, *Finch* (with its dialectal equivalents *Spink* or *Pink*), *Lark*, *Nightingale*, *Pye* (Magpie), *Sparrow*, and *Wildgoose* evince a close and acute observation of the ways of both men and birds on the part of our ancestors.

You will not have read far in your list of names before coming across one of the *Drinkwater* or *Turnbull* type, consisting of a verb with zero ending plus object, unknown in Old English but abounding in modern Romance languages. Our *kerchief*, for instance, is from French *couvre-chef* 'cover-head': the old-fashioned *neckerchief* implied, etymologically, a contradiction in terms. The Norman minstrel who sang the Song of

Roland at the Battle of Hastings bore the name *Taillefer* 'cut-iron', and that Hertfordshire lad of lowly birth who eventually became Pope Adrian IV (1154–9) was known as Nicholas *Breakspeare*. King John was first called *Lackland* by sixteenth-century historians, who thus rendered the *sine terra* and *sans terre* of Latin and French chroniclers. In his sermons the vituperative Hugh Latimer used the current nickname Sir John *Lacklatin* for an ignorant priest and in his pamphlets the polemical Job Throckmorton adopted *Martin Marprelate* as his own pseudonym. The most illustrious of all English names is recorded in the form *Sakspere* (*S-* scribal for *Sh-*) in the Gloucestershire assize rolls for the year 1248 (32 Henry III, roll 274), in the very middle, that is, of the name-giving centuries. According to Ben Jonson, Shakespeare's 'true-filed lines' had the power of 'a lance as brandish'd at the eyes of ignorance', and Thomas Fuller was no less conscious of the form of Shakespeare's name when, in his *Worthies of England*, he likened him to the Roman poet Martial 'in the warlike sound of his surname'. The name *Shakespeare* may be compared with *Shakeshaft*, *Shakelance*, and *Wagstaff*; *Brisbane*, the capital of Queensland in Australia, takes its name from its first governor, Sir T. Makdougall Brisbane (French *briser* 'to break' + Northern English *bane* 'bone'). The first Derbyshire *Copestake* (Yorkshire *Capstick*) was a woodcutter (French *couper* 'to cut' + *stake*) and the first west-country *Boutflower* was a 'bolt-flour' or miller. Besides *Drinkwater* (French *Boileau*) you may recall other verb-object names like *Dolittle*, *Hakluyt* 'hack-little', *Gathercole* (where *cole* may be either 'charcoal' or 'cabbage'), *Lovejoy*, and *Makepeace*.

Owing to lack of adequate evidence, the study of personal nomenclature is beset with many difficulties and uncertainties. The spelling of a family name may have been deliberately changed more than once in its history. Heedless clerks may have perverted it beyond recognition. The surname of the author of *The Pilgrim's Progress*, Bunyan from *Ap-* or

Ab-Annian, a seventh-century Welsh saint, is recorded in thirty-two different spellings. More detailed investigation into English surnames might best be made county by county in collaboration with trained archivists who have full knowledge of extant local documents.

We certainly move on surer ground when we turn to local names. There is scarcely a town or a village in all England that has not at some time given its name to a family. Place-names have an abiding interest: historical, geographical, linguistic, and, above all, human. They may tell us how our ancestors lived and how they looked on life. Place-names may be picturesque, even poetical; or they may be pedestrian, even trivial. All are worthy of observation. As we amble, ramble, cycle, or motor along the lanes of England, we can hardly fail to be lured into diverse reflections as we read the names of villages and farmsteads on the way. Some names mean something to us at once, names like *Ashbourne*, *Castleton*, *Kingsbridge*, *Newhaven*, *Northwood*, and *Orchardleigh*. Others evoke a guess, often a lucky guess. Some knowledge of first principles will help us. Suppose, to take one example only, we bear in mind that characteristic shortening in English of the vowel or diphthong in the first element of a compound, and apply that characteristic to place-names. *Whitacre* and *Whitmore*, it may be reasonably presupposed, show a shortening similar to that in *Whitsunday* from *White Sunday*, and therefore may mean 'white acre or field' and 'white moor' respectively. Compare *break*:*breakfast*; *cave*:*cavern*; *coal*:*collier*; *croup*:*crupper*; *feet*:*fetter* and *fetlock*; *food*:*fodder*; *game*:*gamble*; *good*:*gospel*; *hare*:*harrier*; *heath*:*heather*; *house*:*husband*; *keel*:*kelson*; *know*:*knowledge*; *mead*:*meadow*; *row*:*rowlock*; *sheep*:*shepherd*; *vine*:*vineyard*; and *wise*:*wisdom*. Similarly compare *swine*:*Swinburn* 'pigs' burn or brook' and *goose*:*Gosford* 'goose ford'. Clearly we are safe in interpreting *Cranborne*, *Cranbourne*, *Cranbrook*, and *Cranwell* as 'cranes' stream', *Cranfield* as 'field or open space frequented by cranes', *Cranford* and *Carnforth* as 'cranes' ford', *Cranmere* and *Cranmore* as 'cranes' mere or lake'; *Preston* as 'priests' enclosure', *Prestbury* 'priests' manor', *Presthope* 'priests' hope or valley', *Prestwich* and *Prestwick* 'priests' dairy-farm'; *Shipbourne*, *Shiplake*, and *Shiplate* 'sheep stream, stream where sheep were washed', *Shipden* 'sheep valley', *Shipham* 'sheep homestead', and *Shipmeadow* 'sheep meadow'. In the West Riding we encounter both *Shepley* and *Shipley*, showing earlier and later shortening.

Other examples of shortening may be readily detected in *Acton* 'oak enclosure'; *Bradbourne*, *Bradwall*, and *Bradwell* 'broad stream', *Bradden* 'broad valley', *Bradley* 'broad field or lea', *Bradshaw* 'broad shaw or wood'; *Hampden* 'valley with a homestead', *Hampstead* 'homestead'; *Standen* and *Stanhope* 'stony valley', *Standish* 'stony eddish or pasture', *Standon*, *Stanlawe*, and *Stanlow* 'stony hill', *Stanfield* and *Stanley* 'stony field or lea', and *Stanwell* 'stony spring or stream'. Thousands of names may thus be elucidated with a fair degree of verisimilitude, but if we wish to turn probability into certainty and surmise into proof, we must be prepared to devote much time to serious scientific investigation. Every available recorded form must be studied minutely and an extensive knowledge of many languages and dialects may be required. England is a palimpsest. Names of cities, castles, counties, hundreds, parishes, towns, villages, hamlets, manor houses, farmsteads, inns, roads, lanes, footpaths, bridges, landmarks, mountains, hills, ridges, passes, promontories, cliffs, islands, fields, moors, forests, heaths, rivers, lakes, and streams reveal a variety and wealth of nomenclature unconceived by the casual observer. Some names have long ago passed into oblivion: many names remain obscure and continue to baffle highly trained philologists.

These recorded forms may be found in muniments relating to grants of land, wills, heriots, marriage settlements, leases, mortgages, market and toll rights, manumissions and genealogies, preserved in the British Museum, the Public Record

Office, and county archives; in that Great Inquisition or survey of the lands of England, of their extent, value, ownership, and liabilities, known as Domesday Book, made by order of William the Norman in 1086; and also in assize rolls, diocesan inventories, and parish registers. Having collected all these recorded forms, the investigator arranges them in chronological order. Before attempting to interpret them, however, he must weigh three other no less essential pieces of evidence in the scales of probability: local history, local geography, and modern unsophisticated pronunciation. The history of a place may revolve around a castle, a parish church, a manor house, a market, a bridge, a prehistoric trackway or an ancient well. Does the place stand on the bank of a river, on the shore of a lake, in the middle of a fertile valley, or on a bleak and stony hillside? Every variety of local pronunciation should be carefully registered in narrow phonetic transcription.

Among the commoner village names which survive with relatively little change from Old English times may be noted *Anstey* 'one sty, narrow path', *Aston, Weston, Norton, Sutton, Middleton* or *Milton* 'east, west, north, south, and middle enclosure', *Barton* 'barley enclosure, outlying grange', *Bentley* 'bennet lea, clearing overgrown with coarse, reedy grass', *Bolton* 'manor-house enclosure', *Buckland* 'book land, land held by charter', *Burton* 'fortified enclosure', *Carleton, Charlton* or *Chorlton* 'enclosure of the churls or free peasants', *Chilton* 'enclosure of the children or young noblemen', *Compton* 'enclosure in a coomb or narrow valley', *Denton* 'enclosure in a dean or dale', *Ditton* 'enclosure by a dike or ditch', *Grafton* 'enclosure in or near a grove', *Handley, Hanley, Henley, Healey* or *Heeley* '(at the) high lea or clearing', *Hardwick* 'herd dairy-farm', *Hatfield* 'field or open land where heather grew', *Hatton* 'enclosure on a heath', *Hilton* 'enclosure on a hill', *Hopton* 'enclosure in a hope or valley', *Horton* 'enclosure on muddy land', *Hutton* 'enclosure on the hough, hoe, hoo, or spur of a hill', *Langley* 'long lea or clearing', *Marston* 'enclosure by a marsh', *Marton* 'enclosure by a mere or lake', *Morley* 'moor lea or clearing', *Stratton* or *Stretton* 'enclosure on a Roman road', *Studley* 'clearing for horses', *Swanton* 'enclosure of the swains or swineherds', *Tunstall* 'site of an enclosure', *Waltham* 'homestead in the wold or wood', *Wootton*, *Wotton* 'enclosure in the wood'. Hundreds of villages in our well-watered land grew up near fords across rivers or streams, the first element of the name describing the nature of the crossing: *Greenford* 'green', *Whitford* 'white', *Radford* and *Retford* 'red'; *Defford*, *Deptford*, and *Diptford* 'deep', *Scalford* and *Shadford* 'shallow', *Langford* and *Longford* 'long', *Bradford*, *Romford* and *Widford* 'broad, roomy, and wide', *Darnford*, *Dornford* and *Durnford* 'dern, hidden', *Shereford*, *Sherford* 'sheer, clear', *Freshford* and *Vexford* 'fresh with running water', *Fulford* 'foul, dirty', *Chalford* 'chalky', *Greatford* 'gritty, gravelly', *Sampford* and *Sandford* 'sandy', *Stafford*, *Stamford*, *Stanford*, *Stoford* and *Stowford* 'stony', *Rufford* 'rough', *Ludford* 'loud, by a resounding rapid or waterfall', *Twyford* 'double', *Offord* 'upper of two', *Gainford* 'gain, direct', or *Halliford* 'holy'. Perhaps the ford was distinguished by one particular tree, shrub, or flower: *Alresford* 'alder', *Bramford* 'broom', *Elford* 'elder', *Chagford* 'gorse', *Linford* 'lime, linden', *Guildford* 'marigold', *Oakford*, *Okeford* 'oak', *Salford* 'willow, sallow', or *Wichenford*, *Wishford* and *Witchford* 'wych-elm'. Various animals and birds frequented certain river-crossings and their appellations became permanently attached: *Gateford* 'goat', *Harford*, *Hartford* and *Hertford* 'hart, stag', *Horsford* 'horse', *Tickford* 'kid', *Oxford* 'ox', *Rochford* 'hunting-dog, rache or ratch', *Shefford* and *Shifford* 'sheep', *Swinford* 'pig, swine', *Handford* and *Handforth* 'cock', *Crawford* 'crow', *Enford* 'duck', *Gosford* and *Gosforth* 'goose' and *Ketford* 'kite'. Naturally many fords were named after the rivers over which they led: *Blyford*, over the Blyth; *Dartford*, over the Darent; *Helford*, over the Hayle; *Ilford* in Essex, over the Hyle or Roding; *Ilford* in Somerset, over the Isle; *Kentford*, over the Kennet;

and *Lydford*, over the Lyd. Other fords were named after persons or groups of persons with whom on some notable occasions the way over the stream was linked in memory: *Britford* 'of the brides', *Halford* 'of the hawkers or falconers', *Lattiford* 'of the beggars or vagabonds', *Salterford* 'of the sellers of salt', *Shutford* 'of the shooters or archers', *Thenford* 'of the thanes', *Tetford* and *Thetford* 'of the people, on the public highway'. The ford was situated, perhaps, at or near a well-known landmark: *Chesterford* 'a Roman camp', *Burford* 'a manor house or bury', *Milford* 'a mill', *Stafford* 'a landing-place, stath or staith', *Hainford* 'a park or grove', *Pulford* 'a pool', *Warford* 'a weir', or *Christian Malford* 'a wayside cross'. It was, perhaps, regularly used by travellers on their way to the town of Lynn (*Lynford*) or to the River Thames (*Tempsford*); it may have been crossed by a simple pathway (*Stifford*, *Styford*) or by a Roman road (*Stratford*, *Stretford*, or *Trafford*). Perhaps the ford was used at certain times and seasons: *Efford* 'at ebb-tide', *Barford* 'at the barley harvest', *Heyford* 'at the hay harvest', *Somerford* 'in summer', *Watford* 'in the hunting season', *Mutford* 'when the moot was being held'.

You may have noticed that even in this short list such names as *Stafford* and *Trafford* have appeared more than once with different meanings. The *Stafford* of Staffordshire is the *stæpford* 'the ford by a stath, staith, or landing-place', whereas the East and West *Stafford* in Dorset are so named from *stān ford* 'stone ford'. *Trafford*, in fact, has three possible origins. The three Cheshire *Traffords* (Bridge, Mickle, and Wimbolds) are named from a *trog ford* 'ford in a trough or valley'. The Lancashire *Trafford* near Manchester is merely a Normanized doublet of *Stretford* near by, that is, *strǣt ford* 'ford on a Roman road'. The Northamptonshire *Trafford* in Chipping Warden is manifestly *træppe ford* 'otter-trap ford'. These facts are substantiated by the evidence of well-attested early forms. Other common names of multiple origin are *Broughton*, *Hampton*, *Milton*, *Shirley*, and *Walton*. *Broughton* may mean 'enclosure or farm by a brook' *brōc tūn*; or, like Burton, *burh tūn* 'farm by a bury or fortified manor'; or even *beorg tūn* 'farm by a barrow or hill'. *Hampton* may come from *hām tūn* 'home farm' or from *hamm tūn* 'farm in an inclosed water-meadow', or, quite as frequently, æt *þǣm hēa(ha)n tūne* '(at the) high farm'. Like *Middleton*, *Milton* generally implies 'middle farm'. Nevertheless, the early forms may point definitely to *mylen tūn* 'mill farm'. Shirley has *scīr lēah* as its one Old English antecedent, but the many Shirleys up and down the land must be interpreted variously as 'sheer or bright lea', 'lea belonging to the shire', or 'lea where the shire moot was held', according to circumstances. *Walton* may have four possible interpretations: *Wēala tūn* 'farm of the Britons or of the British slaves'; *weald tūn* 'farm in a weald or on a wold'; *weall tūn* 'farm with a wall or near a (Roman) wall' (Walton in Cumberland actually stands on Hadrian's wall); or, especially in the west country, *wælle tūn* 'farm with a spring or well'.

The scientific investigation of local nomenclature really began in England in the year 1901 when Walter William Skeat published his book on *The Place-Names of Cambridgeshire*. In this and other pioneer studies Skeat was constantly stimulated and encouraged by that erudite scholar Henry Bradley, already mentioned more than once in this book. Skeat and Bradley were soon joined by Sir Allen Mawer, who founded the English Place-Name Society in 1923 under the patronage of the British Academy, and by Sir Frank Stenton of Reading and Professor Eilert Ekwall of Lund. Countless scholars, private students, archivists, librarians, curators, teachers, and schoolchildren have gladly helped in the work of the Society, and as the County Surveys have appeared year by year, notable additions have been made to our knowledge of local archaeology, history, and geography, and of regional dialects past and present.

CHAPTER XIII

British and American English

THE language taken by John Smith to Virginia in 1607 and by the Pilgrim Fathers to Massachusetts in 1620 was the English of Shakespeare and Milton. During the following century and a half most of the colonists who reached the shores of New England were British, but the Dutch founded New Amsterdam and held it until it was seized by the British in 1664 and re-named after the King's brother, the Duke of York. When, in 1790, the thirteen colonies on the Atlantic seaboard ratified the Federal Constitution, they comprised four million English-speaking people, most of whom still dwelt to the east of the Appalachian Mountains. From the linguistic point of view this was the first and decisive stage in the history of United States English, which, by universal consent but less accurately, we call American English for short.

During the period from 1790 to the outbreak of the Civil War in 1860, new States were created west of the Appalachians and the Alleghanies and fresh immigrants arrived in large numbers from Ireland and Germany. The Irish potato famine of 1845 drove one and a half million Irishmen to seek a home in the New World and the European revolution of 1848 caused as many Germans to settle in Pennsylvania and the Middle West.

The third period, from the end of the Civil War in 1865 to the present day, was marked ethnographically by the arrival of Scandinavians, Slavs and Italians. During the closing decades of the nineteenth century one million Scandinavians, or one fifth of the total population of Norway and Sweden, crossed the Atlantic Ocean and settled, for the most part, in Minnesota and in the Upper Mississippi Valley. They were followed by millions of Czechs, Slovaks, Poles, Yugoslavs, and Italians, whose numbers were still further augmented by refugees in flight from the dire political persecutions which degraded Europe in the first half of the twentieth century. As the great American Republic took shape with the attachment of French and Spanish populations, with the addition of native Indian tribes in the Middle West, and with the absorption of Chinese and Japanese who landed on the Pacific Coast, so the cosmopolitan character of the United States became more accentuated. Further, the African Negroes have come to number over ten millions. Never, however, has the language of Washington and Lincoln been in jeopardy. At no time has there threatened any real danger that English might not be capable of completely assimilating the immigrant tongues or that the children of the French in Louisiana, the Germans in Pennsylvania, the Scandinavians in Minnesota, or the Slavs and Italians in Michigan might not all be able to understand, speak, read, and write English in the third and fourth generations.

The literary language, indeed, has seldom diverged perceptibly from that of the homeland. Washington Irving, Edgar Allan Poe and Nathaniel Hawthorne spared no pains in their day to write impeccable standard English. Henry James, Logan Pearsall Smith and Thomas Stearns Eliot were born in America but found an intellectual home in Europe. Edmund Wilson, Elmer Edgar Stoll, George Sherburn, Douglas Bush, and other eminent American critics write not unlike their British models, George Saintsbury, Andrew Cecil Bradley, Oliver Elton, and Sir Herbert Grierson. English literature is now cosmopolitan and worldwide: no sea or ocean bounds can be set to its domain. Henceforth English literature must include all excellent and memorable writing in the

English language, regardless of political and geographical boundaries.

In spelling, vocabulary, and pronunciation, and in the syntax of the lower levels of speech, divergences remain. The distinctive features of American spelling are mainly a legacy bequeathed by that energetic little pale-faced man Noah Webster (1758–1843), whose *American Spelling Book* appeared in 1783 and whose *American Dictionary of the English Language*, the ancestor of all later Webster Dictionaries, was published in 1828. Webster would have liked to effect more drastic reforms in spelling, but he was restrained by necessity. 'Common sense and convenience', he averred, 'would lead me to write *public, favor, nabor, hed, proov, flem, hiz, giv, det, ruf,* and *wel* instead of *publick, favour, neighbour, head, prove, phlegm, his, give, debt, rough,* and *well.*' The practical man of business, however, prevailed over the theoretical reformer. Webster sought a market for his new book on both sides of the Atlantic and he was advised to modify his drastic changes considerably. To-day the second unabridged edition (1934) of Webster's *New International Dictionary* is the official spelling guide of the Government Printing Office and the accepted authority in all American courts. It sanctions such spellings as *-or* for *-our* in *favor, honor, humor, labor, odor,* and *valor* for English *favour, honour, humour, labour, odour,* and *valour*; *-er* for *-re* in *caliber, center, fiber, meter,* and *theater* for English *calibre, centre, fibre, metre,* and *theatre*; one consonant for two in *traveler, traveling, traveled, jewelry,* and *wagon* for English *traveller, travelling, travelled, jewellery,* and *waggon*; *-s-* for *-c-* in the substantives *defense, offense,* and *practise* for English *defence, offence,* and *practice*; various simplifications such as *ax, catalog, check, forever, jail, mask, medieval, program, story, tho, thoro, thru,* and *today* for English *axe, catalogue, cheque, for ever, gaol, masque, mediaeval, programme, storey* (of a building), *though, thorough, through,* and *to-day*. On the analogy, as he thought, of *affection, collection,* and *direction,* Noah Webster clung to *connection* and *reflection* and these spellings are still favoured in America instead of the preferable forms *connexion* and *reflexion*. In general, however, the modified spellings of Webster's Dictionary are sound and sensible. Hundreds of American spellings have won acceptance in England, not only *public* for *publick*, *jail* for *gaol*, *cider* for *cyder*, *asphalt* for *asphalte*, and the like, but also the *-or* spellings for all agent substantives – *author*, *censor*, *conqueror*, *donor*, *juror*, *tailor*, *tutor*, and *visitor* – all, in fact, except *paviour* and *saviour*. The schoolchildren of England are no longer penalized for spelling in the American way and in recent years certain American publishers have deliberately restored a more old-fashioned English spelling.

On arriving in the United States for the first time the Englishman is made unduly aware of differences in vocabulary because these differences happen to loom exceptionally large in the language of travel and transport. Let us assume, by way of illustration, that he decides to continue his journey by rail, that is, by *railroad*. He does not register his luggage but he *checks* his *baggage*, which is then placed, not in the luggage van, but in the *baggage car*; perhaps he must first rescue it from the left-luggage office, which, he discovers, is called the *checkroom*. A goods train is referred to as a *freight train* and a brake-van becomes a *caboose*. He looks for the inquiry office in order to corroborate details and he finds that it is called the *information bureau*; or he may decide to consult a *bulletin-board*, in England a notice-board, or a *schedule*, in England a time-table, on his own account. He is surprised to learn that a season ticket is a *commutation ticket* and that a season-ticket holder is a plain *commuter*. The driver of his train is the *engineer* and the guard is the *conductor*. He hears someone refer to a *switch*, which turns out to be a *point*, and he soon discovers that a *grade crossing* is merely a level crossing. When he reaches his destination he finds an *automobile* waiting for him at the *railroad depot*. He cannot help noticing that the windscreen is called the *windshield*, the bonnet the *hood*, and that petrol is alluded to as *gasoline* or plain *gas*. That explains why the filling station is named the *gas station* and why *accelerating* is described as *stepping on the gas*. On his way through the town he passes trams or *street cars* with their trolley-poles or *contact rods*. He observes cyclists, *cyclers* or *wheelmen*, riding near the pavement or *sidewalk*. One of them has just stopped to mend a puncture or *fix a flat*. Not far away a lorry or *truck* is in difficulties and the breakdown gang or *wrecking crew* is getting to work. Having alighted at his hotel, he finds that it has no personal lift or *elevator* to take him up to his room on the *fifth floor* (which, luckily for him, turns out to be only what he calls the fourth), but that a service lift or *dumbwaiter* may be used for luggage or *baggage*.

At no point is the intelligent traveller inconvenienced by these hitherto unfamiliar, but easily assimilable, expressions. The more difficult task is to understand the living and ever-changing idioms of American slang. Much may be learnt about colloquial and slang idioms from the pages of that intermittent journal *Dialect Notes*, which began its career as long ago as 1890; and from numerous articles appearing in *American Speech*, which was founded as a monthly in 1925, and which now continues to thrive as a quarterly publication of the Columbia University Press. Much, too, may be learnt from the large fourth edition (1936) of Henry Louis Mencken's *The American Language* and its two copious *Supplements* of 1945 and 1948. From *A Dictionary of American English on Historical Principles* (1938–44), by Sir William Craigie and James R. Hulbert, much may be learnt about the 'more serious and solid elements of American English' and about those 'speechways' which mirror the American life of the past. Here, naturally, information may be gleaned about those many trees, shrubs, animals, birds, and reptiles which are rare or unknown in Europe. The countless new arts and techniques of a highly developed civilization figure prominently in its pages, but slang and dialect are restricted to expressions of early date or of

special prominence. Twentieth-century neologisms do not
appear in it at all, for the editors set the year 1900 as their arbitrary time-limit. Since that date many thousands of new words
have become current American and have made their way up
from slang to the more respectable levels of colloquial speech.
'Today', wrote the Baltimore journalist H. L. Mencken in
1945 (*The American Language Supplement One*, p. 323), 'it is no
longer necessary for an American writer to apologize for
writing American. He is not only forgiven if he seeks to set
forth his notions in the plainest and least pedantic manner possible; he is also sure of escaping blame (save, of course, by an
Old Guard of English reviewers) if he makes liberal dips into
the vocabulary of everyday, including its most plausible neologisms. Indeed, he seems a bit stiff and academic if he doesn't
make some attempt, however unhappy, to add to the stock
of such neologisms himself. How many are launched in this
great Republic every year I do not know, but the number
must be formidable. ... So many novelties swarm in that it
is quite impossible for the dictionaries to keep up with them;
indeed, a large number come and go without the lexicographers so much as hearing of them. At least four-fifths of
those which get any sort of toe-hold in the language originate
in the United States, and most of the four-fifths remain here.
We Americans live in an age and society given over to enormous and perhaps even excessive word-making – the most
riotous seen in the world since the break-up of Latin. It is an
extremely wasteful process, for with so many newcomers to
choose from it is inevitable that large numbers of pungent
and useful words and phrases must be discarded and in the end
forgotten by all save linguistic paleontologists. But we must
not complain about that, for all the great processes of nature
are wasteful, and it is by no means assured that the fittest
always survive.' Such neologisms are clipped words like *lube*
for *lubricating oil* and *co-ed* for *co-educational*; back-formations
like *to televise* (1931) from *television* and *to propagand* (1939)

from *propaganda*; blends like *cablegram* from *cable* and *telegram*, *Aframerican* from *African* and *American*, *radiotrician* from *radio* and *electrician*, *sportcast* from *sport* and *broadcast*, and *sneet* from *snow* and *sleet*; artificial or made-up formations like *carborundum*, *cellophane*, and *pianola*; and acronyms or telescoped names like *nabisco* from *National Biscuit Company* or *socony* from *Standard Oil Company*. Hundreds of new expressions have also arisen by a revival and extension of grammatical conversion or the free interchange of function among parts of speech. When we *park* our cars we are using the substantive *park* as a verb in a particular sense. Shakespeare, it is true, used *to park* as a verb in the sense 'to confine or enclose as in a park' in I *Henry the Sixth*, IV. ii. 45: 'How are we park'd and bounded in a pale!' But *to park* in the sense 'to place compactly in a park' was a new conversion made by the British Army in 1812 at the time of the Napoleonic Wars. Nearly one hundred years later, in 1910, it was adopted by British chauffeurs and by American automobilists into their vocabulary. Since then *to park* has come to mean 'to leave or keep other things and persons in a suitable place until required' and Americans park not only their automobiles but also their children, their dogs, and their chewing-gum (P. G. Wodehouse, *The Inimitable Jeeves*). *Stream-line* was first recorded in 1873 in the highly technical language of hydrodynamics. Later, in 1907, it was applied in aerodynamics to the shape given to cars and aircraft offering the minimum resistance to the air. Later still, in 1913, it was converted into the verb *to streamline*, which has recently become a vogue-word in America and has been extended to mean any attempt whatever at simplification. That 'nasty newcomer' *to panic* was used by Thomas Hood in 1827, but apparently by no other writer until it was re-invented in the United States in 1910. To-day Americans no longer hesitate to *loan* (as well as to *lend*), to *audition* (grant a hearing or audition to), to *accession* (new library-books), to *remainder* (unsold and unsalable books), to *service* (a car or an automobile), to *blueprint* (to make any plan of any thing), to *contact* (to get into touch with), to *deadhead* (to admit as a 'deadhead' without payment), to *highlight* (to bring out the brightest parts or chief features of a subject), to *research* (to make researches), to *wastebasket* (to cast as rubbish into the wastepaper-basket), to *air* (to disseminate by radio), to *wax* (to record for the phonograph), and to *brain-trust* (to participate in what we English prefer to call a brains-trust). A bargain is a *good buy*, articles of food are *eats*, and technical skill is the *know-how*.

We refer quite naturally in everyday English to 'children and *grown-ups*' without realizing, perhaps, what an interesting linguistic form the word *grown-ups* is. It is the second or past participle of the intransitive durative verb *grow* (the past participle of which, because durative, has present signification) + the adverb *up*; compounded, converted into a substantive, and given the plural inflexion *-s*. This precise form is not old. It is first recorded in a letter penned by Jane Austen in 1813, although *grown-up* had been used as an epithet adjective in the seventeenth century. When we speak of giving our friends a good *send-off* we are employing an expression first used in this sense of 'a good-will demonstration' by Mark Twain in 1872. Hitherto this verb-adverb substantive had referred to the sending off or starting of contestants in a race. Many other substantives of this type have since found favour in America. A place of concealment is a *hide-out*, a drop in social esteem a *come-down*, a re-organization of staff a *shake-up*, and a free lunch a *hand-out*. Any arrangement or establishment is a *set-up*, a meeting of any kind is a *get-together*, and an escape is a *get-away*. Any action which brings matters to an issue or forces men to disclose their plans is a *show-down* as, at card-games, the players suddenly lay cards on the table. The Americans have a liking, too, for picturesque and vivid verb-phrases, both old and new: *to cut a shine, go the whole hog, shell out, go for, go in for, rope in, go him one better, go it blind, face the music, go it alone, stand from under, do the square thing, knock the* *spots off, spread it on thick, shinny on one's own side, get away with it,* and *paint the town red.* Journalists, gossip-columnists, makers of film and radio scripts, song writers and advertising agents are busy coining new turns of speech day by day. Some of these are literally ephemeral. They do not 'catch on'; they have their day and they are forgotten. Others live on and eventually, perhaps, they are tacitly adopted by the whole English-speaking world.

Suffixes may be resuscitated and multiplied by analogy. In conformity with *mathematician* and *electrician* the old *undertaker*, itself shortened from *funeral undertaker*, becomes *mortician* (1923), not to mention *beautician. Cafeteria* in Spanish is a 'coffee-house': in American English it is extended to mean a 'help-yourself restaurant' and thence proceed *caketeria, fruiteria, groceteria, smoketeria,* and a host of others, some accepted, others transitory, if not merely facetious. On the basis of *sanatorium*, other institutions are named *healthatorium, restatorium,* and *shavatorium.* Thomas Carlyle and others sought to revive the suffix *-dom,* corresponding to German *-tum,* in the nineteenth century and among their creations that survived were *boredom, officialdom,* and *serfdom.* Hundreds of new *-dom* compounds – *filmdom, stardom, crosswordpuzzledom, dictatordom, gangsterdom,* and *slumdom* – are now fashionable in America. The ancient agent suffixes, Greek *-ist* and Germanic *-ster,* have likewise come to life again in *vacationist* (holiday-maker, 1888), *manicurist* (1889), *behaviorist* (coined by John B. Watson in 1913), *receptionist* (1923), *blurbist* (concocter of blurbs or slip-cover encomiums, 1925), and *editorialist* (1944); *ringster* (1879), *gangster* (1896), *roadster* (1910), and *speedster* (1918).

Among the more outstanding features of American pronunciation a few may here be noted. In words like *for, door, farm,* and *lord* the *r* is still sounded as a fricative, whereas in English it is silent except in expressions like *far away* and *the door opens* where a linking *r* is naturally inserted. In most dialects of Southern England the rolled or trilled *r* sound was weakened in pronunciation in the seventeenth century and lost in the eighteenth. Americans pronounce words like *dance*, *fast*, *grass*, *half*, and *path* with a low front *a* sound [æ] as in *cat*, which is still heard in the northern counties of England and which persisted in the southern counties until the end of the eighteenth century. Americans pronounce words like *dock*, *fog*, *hot*, and *rod* with a low back *a* sound [ɑ] like the vowel sound in *car* and *father* shortened. They pronounce words like *dew*, *duke*, *new*, and *steward* with the [ju:] sound reduced to [u:] so that *dew* and *duke* sound like *do* and *dook*. Just as in Spanish, Portuguese and Provençal, the Latin and Italian *armata*, past participle feminine, 'armed (force)', has become *armada*, so in present-day American -*t*- is often voiced, so that *beating* sounds very much like *beading*, *matter* like *madder*, and *metal* like *medal*. The plosion, however, is softer and less aspirated than in English.

Further, it may be noted that both word-stress and sentence-stress are weaker in American than in British English and intonation is more level. Consequently American speech is more monotonous, but at the same time it is generally more distinct. It is, as Mencken puts it, 'predominantly *staccato* and *marcato*', whereas British English, like Russian, 'tends towards *glissando*'. Unstressed syllables are pronounced with more measured detachment and therefore with greater clarity. There is less variety of tone and the customary tempo is slower. Many speakers have fallen into a habit which they have unconsciously inherited from seventeenth-century East Anglian Puritans. They allow the soft palate or velum to droop while speaking, and as a result part of the breath stream passes through the nose giving a certain nasalized quality or 'nasal twang' to vowel sounds which may vary considerably in degree from individual to individual.

Compare the way in which a New Yorker says *extra-ordinary*, *supernumerary*, *temporary*, and *unexceptionable* with the pronunciation of a Londoner. The American invariably gives to the unstressed syllables in these words greater 'prominence' (to use the technical term in phonetics) and, consequently, greater audibility. In words like *dormitory, monastery, necessary,* and *secretary* he habitually places a not unpleasing secondary stress upon the penult or last syllable but one. Some words he stresses differently from us. He stresses *aristocrat, detail, eczema, frontier, harass, primarily,* and *subaltern* on the second syllable whereas we stress them on the first. Conversely, he stresses *address, alloy, ally, corollary, defect, idea, inquiry, opponent, quinine, recess, recourse, redress, research, resource,* and *romance* on the first syllable, whereas we English stress them on the second. Other words, like *advertisement* and *financier,* are stressed on the second syllable in London but on the third syllable in New York.

Now these observations apply not only to the speech of New York City but also to the so-called General American dialect as a whole, which includes the Middle Atlantic States, that is, New Jersey, Pennsylvania and the whole of New York State west of the Hudson River, as well as all the Middle and Western States. General American thus comprises two-thirds of the whole population and four-fifths of the land surface of the United States reaching from the Atlantic Ocean in the east to the Pacific Ocean in the west. The other two dialects, New England and Southern, are important and significant, but they are much more limited. The dialect of New England is spoken in Maine, New Hampshire, Vermont, Massachusetts, Rhode Island, Connecticut, and the strip of New York State lying to the east of the Hudson River. It is nearer British English in many respects. For example, the rounded vowel is retained in *dock,* the long low back *a* is heard in *dance* and the *r* is dropped in *far* and *farm.* At the same time, it is less homogeneous than General American. Even within its narrower confines the New England dialect has far more social and regional variations. The Southern dialect includes the States of Maryland, Virginia, North and South

Carolina, Georgia, Florida, Kentucky, Tennessee, Alabama, Mississippi, Arkansas, and Louisiana, as well as a great part of Missouri, Oklahoma, and Texas. In other words, it is spoken in all the States, except Delaware and West Virginia, lying south of Pennsylvania and the Ohio River and east of a line running from St Louis to the middle waters of the Colorado River and thence down that river to its mouth in the Gulf of Mexico. Many people in these parts speak with a drawl. They speak with slow enunciation and they frequently drag out and diphthongize stressed vowels, saying [jeɪs], or even [jeɪjəs], for *yes*, and [klæɪs], or even [klæɪjəs], for *class*.

In spite of countless smaller variations in pronunciation, vocabulary, and idiom, the three American dialects do not greatly differ from one another. For two centuries and more American families have been constantly on the move: speech communities have seldom been isolated for more than one generation. It would be no exaggeration to say that greater differences in pronunciation are discernible among the speech-forms of Northern England between Trent and Tweed than among the dialects of the whole of North America.

It is now customary for American and British scholars and scientists to co-operate in the writing of composite books addressed to the whole English-speaking world and the councils of learned societies have taken steps to standardize technical nomenclature. Other potent forces are now at work bringing the two main streams of English more closely together. Future historians of our language, with their longer perspective in looking back, may well record that it was during the century and a quarter from 1800 to 1925 that British and American English showed the greatest divergence and that, after 1925, unifying factors - the ubiquity of radio and the interchange of films, novels, journals, and plays - all worked in one and the same direction to make that divergence narrower and narrower. Films and newspapers bring the latest American slang to England, so that even a trained observer may no longer differentiate with certainty between native and imported neologisms. Such a highly expressive phrase as *It's up to us* sounds so very American. We take it for granted that it *is* American. But who could be really certain about its provenance without looking a little more closely into the matter, without consulting Mencken, Horwill and *American Speech* on the one hand, and Partridge and the Supplement to *The Oxford English Dictionary* on the other? In 1942 the United States War Department furnished men and women serving in Europe with *A Short Guide to Great Britain* which included a long list of American and English variants. It was a painstaking, if over-elaborate, publication: its aim – to obviate every conceivable occasion of misapprehension – was entirely meritorious. This aim was shared by H. W. Horwill in his two careful studies which had appeared a few years previously and which have already acquired historical value : *A Dictionary of Modern American Usage* (1935) and *An Anglo-American Interpreter* (1939). In his Preface to the last-mentioned book the author quotes the statement of a 'distinguished journalist' that 'an American, if taken suddenly ill while on a visit to London, might die in the street through being unable to make himself understood. ... He would naturally ask for the nearest drugstore, and no one would know what he meant.' Everyone would now know the meaning of this and hundreds of other expressions marked American in Horwill's *Interpreter* and in the War Department's *Short Guide*. Indeed, they may now be heard from the lips of English children every day. The most fashionable American locution of the hour may be heard all over England within the space of a few weeks and then, perhaps, heard no more.

CHAPTER XIV

Tendencies and Trends

It is a notable fact that the inflexions of present-day English are substantially the same as they were in Shakespeare's time. Since then there have been only slight losses, such as that of *-est* and *-eth* in the second and third persons singular present of the verb. Further structural simplification is hardly likely to be continued. Is it conceivable, for example, that the *-s* in *he comes* will one day be dropped on the analogy of *come* in all the other forms of the present? This would bring English into line with Danish, which, according to Otto Jespersen, is in this particular respect more 'advanced' than English. Certainly *he come* is heard in many dialects and in many sub-standard forms of English. The revival of the subjunctive in 'I demand that he come', which is gaining ground in America over the more usual subjunctive substitute 'that he should come', may point to a tendency, however vague and ill defined, for the language to move in this direction and to shed 'the chief of consonants' in this position. Turning to the pronouns, we observe that *thou*, *thee*, and *thine* have been discarded since Milton's day except in dialectal, archaic, and liturgical usage; that *ye* has been supplanted by *you* in everyday speech, but that the differences between subjective *I* and objective *me*, *he* and *him*, *she* and *her*, *we* and *us*, *they* and *them*, are well maintained in standard speech although these formal distinctions are no more necessary in pronouns than in substantives. If one form of a substantive may now serve as either subject or object, according to its position, in the same way one pronoun might be generalized. But all these pronominal forms are monosyllabic, they are in frequent use, and they are capable of bearing the main stress. They have therefore escaped the levelling process. *Whom*, on the other hand, is in a different plight. At the conversational level it has gone and it is unstable elsewhere. As a relative, *who* is parallel to *that* and *which* and, as an interrogative, to *what*; *that*, *which* and *what* have been uninflected for centuries. In spite of the heavy weight of conservative tradition supporting it, the distinction between *who* and *whom* has become more and more enfeebled in recent years.

The complex structure of our language is the outcome of centuries of steady growth and yet attempts might be made to remedy deficiencies in its mechanism. It might be argued, for example, that English would be improved as a medium of communication by the adoption of a common or epicene pronoun which might refer clearly and definitely to both male and female. Such a phrase as 'Everyone to their liking' is manifestly unsatisfactory. It deserves to be branded as a solecism, and yet it answers a real need in that it shows beyond all possible doubt that women are also included in this observation. Historically gender is not to be identified with sex. By agelong convention 'he' includes 'she', and yet precise philosophical writers deem it necessary continually to be reminding their readers of this elementary fact by means of footnotes and other devices. 'Everyone to his liking' is now felt to be not definite enough, and 'Everyone to his or her liking' is unnatural and cumbersome. In this particular instance the inherited mechanism of French is far more satisfactory. 'Chacun à son goût' admits of no possible ambiguity since masculine *son* refers to the grammatical gender of *goût* and not to the sex of *chacun*. But 'Everybody has their level' may be encountered even in Jane Austen's *Emma*.

The mechanism of the English language would also be improved by the adoption or invention of some indefinite

pronoun other than *one* to correspond in meaning and usage
to French *on*, deriving from Latin *homo, hominem* 'man', and to
German *man*, which is readily distinguishable from *der Mann*
both in speech (because, like *man* in the Scandinavian languages and like *men* in Dutch, it is pronounced with weaker
stress and with reduced vowel) and in writing (since it has one
final *n* and no initial capital). The English *one* is overworked:
as a universal indefinite pronoun it is hardly satisfactory. 'One
never knows, does one?' 'One cannot always foresee one's
needs when one travels.' Sometimes 'a man' is preferable, as
in Francis Bacon's well-known epigram, 'A man is but what
he knoweth': but then Bacon was writing with the memory
of Latin in his mind. He was not flagrantly excluding women
from knowledge! To ask a plain, simple question is the primal
right of all human beings (or 'of all humans' as the Americans
do not hesitate to say) or, in the words of the old proverb, 'A
man may speer the gate to Rome'. 'A man may drink and no
be drunk', said Robert Burns, echoed by Sir Walter Scott. 'A
man's reach should exceed his grasp', declaimed Browning in
Andrea del Sarto. 'A fellow' is more colloquial: 'What else can
a fellow do?' 'You' is more intimate: 'You never can tell.'
But 'you', like 'we' and 'they', may be ambiguous. In the end
the already overburdened passive voice may be used.

In the present century the English language is being constantly subjected to stresses and strains. Apart from slang, the
jargon of technology and the crude lingo of newspaper headlines tug away from the centre violently and dangerously.
The language of the technical and technological sciences tends
to be esoteric and, at the same time, international. In order to
make his article intelligible to his fellow-researchers, the writer
may find it necessary to define his terms as he goes along. He
may have no knowledge of or interest in the art of verbal presentation: his professional colleagues will, he hopes, meet him
half way or more than half way. In a foreign technical periodical the summary or résumé accompanying an article or dis-

sertation may be printed in English as well as in other world languages, like French, Spanish, and Russian. The purpose of this abstract is to give the substance of the dissertation in the briefest possible space so that investigators in the same field may ascertain at a glance how far the new discoveries have any bearing on their own work. The standard of this particular form of 'international language' varies considerably, but it may be so low that the most accommodating and attentive reader may find himself going over a sentence many times before apprehending its meaning and he may be driven, in the last resort, to translate a sentence or clause into the author's own mother tongue in order to elicit such meaning as it may have.

We may compare the linguistic crudity of so many technological epitomes with that of journalistic headlines, film captions, and advertisements. Amidst the clack and clatter of the modern world many readers of newspapers 'skim the headlines' first of all and then dip into an article here and there as the whim takes them. From pressure of business or from lack of concentration they may content themselves with perusing the headlines alone and relying upon them entirely for their knowledge of what is going on in the world. The drafting of the headline therefore constitutes a most important part of journalistic technique. No longer a mere title or label, the headline must itself convey information direct. It must convey that information as briefly as possible. As the type assumes larger and larger proportions, so the number of letters and spaces is more strictly limited. The broad letters m and w are certainly not in favour. Words cannot be conveniently divided at the end of the line. The short words, not the right words, must be sought at all costs. The all-powerful headline-men soon reduced the North Atlantic Treaty of 1949 to the lower status of a pact and very soon the Secretary of State for Foreign Affairs was himself heard talking about the North Atlantic Pact in the House of Commons. Indeed, in the language of headlines, any compact, contract, agreement, engagement, convention, covenant, stipulation, armistice, pledge, truce, or treaty becomes a *pact*; just as any experienced or proficient person in any capacity whatsoever becomes an *ace*; any interdict or prohibition, a *ban*; any offer or attempt, a *bid*; any superintendent, supervisor, overseer, governor, manager, director, or commander, a *chief*; any abridgement, abbreviation, shortening, curtailment or reduction, a *cut*; any negotiation, transaction, or bargain, a *deal*; any concerted or co-ordinated public effort, a *drive*; any proclamation, declaration, regulation, ordinance, or enactment, an *edict*; any ambassador, representative, delegate, intermediary, intercessor, mediator, go-between, minister, nuncio, or herald, an *envoy*; any undertaking, piece of work, enterprise, achievement, performance, occupation, profession, employment, affair, concern, or task, a *job*; any assembly, convention, congregation, conference, conclave, synod, or meeting, a *meet*; any supplication, petition, application, entreaty, appeal, or request, a *plea*; any investigation, interrogation, examination, scrutiny, inquiry, or inquest, a *probe*; any disagreement, controversy, contention, altercation, dissension, dispute, squabble, or discord, a *row*; any unexpected obstacle, sudden difficulty, unforeseen impediment, hindrance, hitch, or check, a *snag*; any address, oration, lecture, monologue, harangue, palaver, discourse, or speech, a *talk*; and any endeavour, experiment, attempt, effort, essay, trial, or test, a *try*. The copy-reader will naturally prefer back-formations to compounds, he will clip words wherever he can and, disregarding current syntax, he will lop sentences without mercy. When Professor Sir William Craigie was invited to join the staff of the Department of English in the University of Chicago with a view to directing the compilation of *The Dictionary of American English*, his acceptance was duly announced by an article in *The Chicago Tribune* on October 18, 1924, which bore the headline:

MIDWAY SIGNS LIMEY PROF TO DOPE YANK TALK

By the figure of speech known as synecdoche *Midway* means Chicago, since Midway Plaisance is the name of the boulevard area connecting Washington and Jackson Parks in that city. *Limey* is a slang term for a British sailor or *lime-juicer*, who, according to report, drinks lime-juice as an anti-scorbutic. *Yank* or *Yankee*, it may be added, comes from the Dutch for *Little Jan* or *John* and is an old American Indian nickname for a New England sailor. 'Chicago appoints a British Professor to diagnose (interpret) American speech' might stand as a possible interpretation or translation of this typical eight-word headline. G. K. Chesterton, writing only a few years later, declared that linguistic deterioration would result from 'that passion for compression and compact information which possesses so many ingenious minds in America. Everyone can see how an entirely new system of grammar, syntax, and even language has been invented to fit the brevity of headlines. Such brevity, so far from being the soul of wit, is even the death of meaning; and certainly the death of logic.' My eyes have just lighted on this good specimen of telegraphese in to-day's *Liverpool Daily Post*:

COMMUNISTS FEAR SPLIT GERMANY BLAME

In other words, 'The Communists fear that they may be blamed for splitting Germany'.

Max Müller, Wilhelm Wundt, Barrett Wendell, and many others, as evidence of the poverty of the average working man's vocabulary, were too fond of quoting Dean Farrar, who alleged that he had once 'listened for a long time together to the conversation of three peasants who were gathering apples among the boughs of an orchard and, as far as I could conjecture, the whole number of words they used did not exceed a hundred'. The Dean's testimony, in fact, had little scientific validity. His observation was just casual. His conjecture was a conjecture and nothing more. In different circumstances the word store of an observant and intelligent farm-labourer might be both rich and varied, whereas, on the other hand, that of a well-informed and well-educated townsman might be amazingly meagre. Only a man with a vigorous and alert mind is capable of wielding a large vocabulary effectively, observing the finer distinctions between words correctly, and keeping his linguistic tools furbished and bright. A narrowly restricted vocabulary, whether the outcome of ignorance, sloth, or deliberate artificial limitation, must imply an entirely unnecessary stretching and straining of the structure of speech. English has the richest vocabulary in the world, two hundred thousand words, apart from compounds and derivatives, being in current use. For the past thousand years our language has opened its doors widely to visiting words and it has offered permanent hospitality to many. With differing shades of emphasis I may, for example, express the simple concept of wishing or velleity in a pleasing variety of ways: I *wish, long, yearn, should like, would fain, have a mind* from Old English; I *crave for, want* from Old Norse; I *hanker after* from Flemish; I *desire, aspire after* from Latin through French; I *desiderate* from the past participle of Latin *dēsīderāre* direct. Next to Latin, French, Scandinavian, and Greek, our vocabulary owes most to Italian, whose beneficent influence began with Chaucer and reached its zenith in the sixteenth century. From Italian we have taken numerous expressions relating to architecture (*cupola, pedestal, pilaster, piazza, belvedere, portico, balcony, corridor,* and *pergola*), to art (*relief, virtuoso, bust, profile, vista, attitude,* and *filigree*), to literature (*buffoon, sonnet, stanza, canto, burlesque,* and *pasquinade*), and, above all, to music (*madrigal, opera, serenade, sonata, solo, cantata,* and *oratorio,* not to mention all the various terms for technical directions and the names of instruments). Spanish guests were likewise welcomed at the Renaissance: commercial terms like *anchovy, cask,* and *sherry*; naval and military terms like *armada, galleon, ambuscade,* and *comrade*; as well as *banana, cannibal, mosquito, Negro,* and *potato* from across the Atlantic. Then, too, *cambric, hawker, muff,* and *scone* found their way into the speech of commerce from Dutch and Low German; *dock, freebooter, monsoon, reef*, and *yacht* as maritime terms, and other more general terms like *furlough, knapsack, onslaught, uproar, mart* (forming a doublet with *market* from French) and *waggon* (forming a doublet with *wain* from Old English). The Russian words *tsar, kvass, moujik, rouble*, and *verst* date from the time of Richard Chancellor's voyages in search of a north-east passage to India in 1553 and the institution of the Muscovy Trading Company under Queen Elizabeth. To-day we are familiar with such words as *almanac, arsenal, calibre, cipher, cotton, nadir, zenith*, and *zero* from Arabic; *bungalow, dinghy, loot*, and *pyjamas* from Hindi; *azure, bazaar, caravan, chess, paradise, scarlet*, and *tiger* from Persian; *coffee, fez, horde, kiosk, tulip*, and *turban* from Turkish; *atoll, calico, curry*, and *teak* from Dravidian; *silk* and *tea* from Tibeto-Chinese; *bamboo, gutta-percha*, and *sago* from Malay; *taboo* and *tattoo* from Polynesian; *hammock* and *hurricane* from Caribbean through Spanish; *maize* from Cuban; and *igloo* from Eskimo.

It was an odd coincidence by which the initial letters of the names of King Charles II's ministers, Clifford, Arlington, Buckingham, Ashley (Earl of Shaftesbury), and Lauderdale, spelled the word *cabal*, meaning 'clique or faction', of ancient Hebrew origin. To-day we all have to familiarize ourselves with countless similar initial-letter coinages, whether we approve of them or not. From the full name to the simplified label three stages may be detected. For example, the Society for Checking the Abuses of Public Advertising becomes first S.C.A.P.A., then SCAPA, and finally Scapa. In the interests of the perplexed reader this last stage may well be discouraged, since thereby the abbreviation is made unnecessarily cryptic. As we move about in the modern world we hear people calling the Association of Special Libraries and Information Bureaux, ASLIB; the Council for the Encouragement of Music and the Arts, CEMA; the Entertainments National

Service Association, ENSA; the Fabrica Italiana Automobile Torino, FIAT; the Club for Poets, Playwrights, Essayists, Editors and Novelists, the PEN Club; and Political and Economic Planning, PEP. UNESCO, the United Nations Educational Scientific and Cultural Organization, is one of the eleven specialized agencies of UNO, the United Nations Organization. UNESCO was first christened UNECO when it was formed as an 'international educational agency' by the Conference of Allied Ministers in 1942. Three years later it was realized that 'only in a loose and broad sense could culture be taken to include science, especially applied science'. The additional qualifier 'scientific' was therefore inserted. In ordinary discourse we spell out the letters of unpronounceable alphabeticisms. We speak of the C.E.W.C. for the Council for Education in World Citizenship, the C.P.R.E. for the Council for the Preservation of Rural England, the L.S.O. for the London Symphony Orchestra and the W.E.A. for the Workers' Educational Association. The student of literature has his own long list of abbreviations to master. He must, for instance, distinguish at once between the *B.N.B.*, *The British National Bibliography*, and the *D.N.B.*, *The Dictionary of National Biography*; between the *C.H.E.L.*, *The Cambridge History of English Literature* and the *C.S.E.L.*, *Corpus Scriptorum Ecclesiasticorum Latinorum*. Many abbreviations are so seldom expanded that their precise significations are forgotten. T.B. stands for Tubercle Bacillus: G.I. for General Issue. M and B are the initials of May and Baker, the manufacturers of that important curative drug M and B 693. Abbreviations are not always time-savers: they may become linguistic pests. At best they are N.Ns., necessary nuisances. We have, it is true, numerous (and expensive) *Dictionaries of Abbreviations* to help us in our difficulties, but too many of these are hastily compiled, incomplete and inaccurate. In any case, they are no sooner published than they are out of date. Like slang, abbreviations may be of short life. They are shadowy and inhuman devices appearing and disappearing in that strange border country which separates speech from the mathematical sciences.

Our language is ever adapting itself to changing circumstances. It is slowly shifting from day to day. The vigilant observer can detect its drift and slope. Now and then he discerns trends and tendencies which seem to him to adumbrate or prefigure the modifications of the next few centuries. He sees a resuscitation of synthetic processes, especially in the use of prefixes and suffixes. The English sentence is still growing in importance at the expense of the word. At the same time, there is a drift towards the invariable word. Our language is rich in diphthongs, but many are unstable: they are slowly but surely being transmuted on the lips of the young. Diphthongs tend to become simple long vowels or monophthongs: long vowels tend to be shortened. Not only in America but also in Britain, breathed or voiceless consonants are liable to become voiced. Plosives are liable to become fricatives.

English is now spoken as the first or mother tongue by over two hundred millions of people and it is read and understood by many millions more. Its influence, too, upon other languages is considerable, and yet – it is important to remind ourselves of this fact – that influence is surprisingly recent. It was not until the eighteenth century, when it was already mature, that English exerted any really appreciable influence on other national tongues.

The four million speakers of the five distinctive Middle English dialects were reduced to little more than half that number by the mortal ravages of the Black Death which afflicted the towns and villages of England in the time of Chaucer and Wyclif. Shakespeare wrote his plays in the language of five and a half million people, in a language which then held fifth place in the Western hemisphere, for it was far exceeded in the number of its speakers by French, German, Italian, and Spanish. French remained the first language of

Europe until the Napoleonic Wars when it was surpassed by German. Throughout the remainder of the nineteenth century German retained first place in Europe, but in the fourth and fifth decades of the twentieth century it was exceeded in the number of its speakers by Russian. Meantime, however, by the middle of the nineteenth century, English, while remaining the second language in Europe, had become the first language in the world.

Until the seventeenth century, when the author of *Paradise Lost* served as one of Cromwell's political secretaries, Latin was still the official language of European diplomacy. It was in the reign (1643–1715) of the Grand Monarch, Louis XIV, that French, the most precise and lucid of all living tongues, superseded Latin as the recognized medium of international negotiations. This was brought about by a fortunate combination of circumstances, and the disinterested philologist, whatever his nationality, cannot fail to deplore the declining part played by the French language in world diplomacy since the formulation of the Treaty of Versailles in 1919. Was it not symbolic that, at those momentous councils, Woodrow Wilson and Lloyd George could speak little French, but Georges Clemenceau expressed himself in English with easy fluency? To-day, thanks to a highly developed mechanical technique, international conferences are conducted simultaneously in three or four world languages.

English is likely to remain the most widespread language in the world but its future largely depends upon the energy and enterprise of the people who speak it. Other great languages are consolidating themselves with remarkable rapidity, notably Russian and Chinese. Russian is the official language of the Soviet Union with its 135 millions of inhabitants in Europe and its 45 millions in Asia. Gwoyeu, the national tongue of China, based primarily upon the spoken North Mandarin dialect in its Peiping variety, is now estimated to be the accepted official language of 280 millions of Chinese. Upon Russian,

Chinese, Spanish and other widely spoken languages the impact of English is probably stronger than ever and in those urgent tasks which now confront mankind as a whole – the evolution of a supranational government and the redintegration of philosophy, science, and religion – our language is manifestly ordained to assume a prominent role. As in the past, so in the future, it will shape and adapt itself unceasingly to meet new needs, and in that incessant reshaping and adaptation every speaker and writer, consciously or unconsciously, will play some part.

FOR FURTHER READING

CHAPTER I

OF the many surveys of the history of the English language those by
Bradley and Jespersen are still the most stimulating: Henry Bradley,
The Making of English, London (Macmillan), 1904, 250 pp.; and Otto
Jespersen, *Growth and Structure of the English Language*, Oxford
(Blackwell), 1905, 255 pp. No less readable are the brief histories by
Smith, Wrenn, Pei, and Brook: Logan Pearsall Smith, *The English
Language*, Oxford University Press, re-issued with an Epilogue by
Robert William Chapman, 1952, 286 pp.; Charles Leslie Wrenn, *The
English Language*, London (Methuen), 1949, 236 pp.; Mario Pei, *The
Story of English*, London (Allen and Unwin), 1953, 381 pp.; and
George Leslie Brook, *A History of the English Language*, London
(Deutsch), 1958, 224 pp. Henry Cecil Wyld's *The Historical Study of
the Mother Tongue, An Introduction to Philological Method*, London
(Murray), 1906, xi+412 pp., is probably the most instructive of all
his books, which also include *A Short History of English*, London
(Murray), third edition 1927, viii+294 pp., and *A History of Modern
Colloquial English*, Oxford (Blackwell), third edition 1936, xviii+
433 pp. Albert Croll Baugh's *A History of the English Language*, New
York (Appleton-Century), second edition 1961, 804 pp., gives a comprehensive survey, laying special emphasis on 'external history'; and
to each of its eleven chapters a full critical bibliography is appended.
Three other American books may also be strongly recommended,
namely George Harley McKnight and Bert Emsley's *Modern English
in the Making*, New York (Macmillan), 1928, 590 pp.; Albert H.
Marckwardt's *Introduction to the English Language*, Oxford University
Press, 1942, xvii+347 pp.; and Stuart Robertson and Frederic Cas-
sidy's *The Development of Modern English*, London (Harrap), 1954,
478 pp. A magistral essay on *The English Language* has been contributed by Charles Talbut Onions to *The Character of England* (pp. 280-
302), edited by Sir Ernest Barker, Oxford University Press, 1947.
Fernand Mossé's *Esquisse d'une histoire de la langue anglaise*, Paris

(IAC), 1947, xv+ 268 pp., is both lucid and profound. Karl Brunner's *Die englische Sprache: ihre geschichtliche Entwicklung*, Halle (Niemeyer), second edition 1961, 804 pp., is indispensable to advanced students.

An attractive initiation into Indo-European philology is offered by Antoine Meillet in his *Introduction a l'étude comparative des langues indoeuropéennes*, Paris (Hachette), eighth edition 1937, xxvi+ 502 pp. The same author's introduction to Germanic, *Caractères généraux des langues germaniques*, Paris (Hachette), fourth edition 1930, xvi+ 236 pp., may be studied side by side with Hermann Hirt's *Handbuch des Urgermanischen*, 3 volumes, Heidelberg (Winter), 1931–4. Thomas Hudson Williams, *A Short Introduction to the Study of Comparative Grammar (Indo-European)*, Cardiff (University of Wales Press), 1935, xii+ 78 pp., is a neat and useful booklet. The most advanced book on Germanic in English is Edward Prokosch, *A Comparative Germanic Grammar*, Philadelphia (Pennsylvania University Press), 1939, 353 pp. An excellent introduction is also provided by the first three chapters of William Edward Collinson and Robert Priebsch's *The German Language*, London (Faber), fourth edition 1958, in the Great Languages series.

CHAPTER II

Sir Frank Stenton's *Anglo-Saxon England*, Oxford University Press, second edition 1955, 748 pp., forming the second volume of *The Oxford History of England*, contains a full critical bibliography. R. H. Hodgkin's *A History of the Anglo-Saxons*, Oxford University Press, third edition 1953, two volumes, 840 pp., dealing only with the periods before King Alfred's death, is richly illustrated by pictures, facsimiles, and maps. Peter Hunter Blair's *An Introduction to Anglo-Saxon England*, Cambridge University Press, 1956, xvi+ 382 pp., describes various aspects of our early culture. The prehistoric and ethnographic backgrounds are well portrayed by Hector Munro Chadwick in his profound studies, *The Origin of the English Nation*, Cambridge University Press, 1907, 332 pp., and *The Heroic Age*, Cambridge University Press, 1912, 474 pp. Dorothy Whitelock's *The Beginnings of English Society*, Pelican Books, 1952, 256 pp., provides an admirable account of this subject written for the general reader.

Excellent introductions to the Old English language are provided by George Leslie Brook, *An Introduction to Old English,* Manchester University Press, 1955, xi+138 pp., and by Randolph Quirk and C. L. Wrenn, *An Old English Grammar*, London (Methuen), 1955, ix+166 pp. Older text-books are still valuable: Joseph and Elizabeth Mary Wright, *Old English Grammar*, Oxford University Press, 1908, 372 pp.; and its abridged version, *An Elementary Old English Grammar*, 1923, 192 pp. The most fully documented descriptions are those by Sievers-Brunner and Campbell: Karl Brunner, *Altenglische Grammatik nach der angelsächsischen Grammatik von Eduard Sievers neubearbeitet*, Halle (Niemeyer), second edition 1951, x+449 pp.; and Alistair Campbell, *Old English Grammar*, Oxford University Press, 1959, 436 pp. Henry Sweet's *Anglo-Saxon Reader*, Oxford, first edition 1876, frequently revised by Charles Talbut Onions, is a classic of its kind. So, too, is *Sweet's Anglo-Saxon Primer*, Oxford, ninth edition, viii+129 pp., designed as an introduction to the *Reader*, and now revised by Norman Davis.

CHAPTER III

The Viking invasions are well described by Sir Thomas Downing Kendrick in *A History of the Vikings*, London 1930, 412 pp., and by Hodgkin (p. 473 ff.), Stenton (p. 237 ff.), and Blair (p. 55 ff.) in the books mentioned above. A shorter sketch is given by Sir Allen Mawer in *The Vikings*, Cambridge University Press, 1913, 150 pp. Sir Frank Stenton's Raleigh Lectures, *The Danes in England*, published in the Proceedings of the British Academy, Vol. xiii, 1927, are fresh and illuminating. Gabriel Turville-Petre gives a good introduction to Scandinavian history in *The Heroic Age of Scandinavia*, London (Hutchinson), 1951, viii+196 pp. Erik Björkman's pioneering studies are now classics: *Scandinavian Loan-words in Middle English*, Halle (Niemeyer), 1900–1902, 360 pp., and *Nordische Personennamen in England in alt-und früh-mittelenglischer Zeit*, Halle (Niemeyer), 1910. E. V. Gordon's *An Introduction to Old Norse*, Oxford University Press, second edition 1957, 384 pp., contains a valuable Appendix on *The Old Norse Tongue in England*; and his translation of Haakon Shetelig and Hjalmar Falk's *Scandinavian Archaeology*, Oxford University Press, 1937, 458 pp., is enriched by original footnotes.

P. van Dyke Shelly's *English and French in England,* 1066–1100, Philadelphia, 1921, gives a clear account of the rivalry between the two languages. So, too, does R. M. Wilson's highly informative essay on the later struggle, *English and French in England, 1100–1300,* contributed to *History,* Vol. 28, 1943, p. 37 ff. The standard manual of Anglo-Norman is that by Johan Vising (1855–1942) of the University of Göteborg: *Anglo-Norman Language and Literature,* Oxford University Press, 1923, 112 pp., which should be studied in conjunction with the publications of the Anglo-Norman Text Society, founded in 1936. The study by Mary Dominica Legge, *Anglo-Norman in the Cloisters,* Edinburgh University Press, 1950, vii+147 pp., is concerned with French writing on this side of the Channel 'when all England was bilingual, and much of it was trilingual'. Readers of French will consult Tome II of René Huchon's *Histoire de la langue anglaise, 1066–1475,* Paris 1930, vii+392 pp., as well as Tome I of Ferdinand Brunot's monumental *Histoire de la langue française,* Paris, 1905, especially Chapitre IX, *Le Français à l'étranger;* Albert Dauzat's more concise *Histoire de la langue française,* Paris, 1930, 588 pp.; and E. Walberg's *Quelques Aspects de la littérature anglo-normande,* Paris, 1936. Mildred Pope's treatise *From Latin to Modern French with especial consideration of Anglo-Norman,* Manchester University Press, 1934, 572 pp., contains a long chapter, pp. 420–85, on the development of the French language in England. John Orr's Taylorian Lecture, *The Impact of French upon English,* Oxford, 1948, 28 pp., is entertaining. For both Scandinavian and French borrowings the reader will consult Mary Sydney Serjeantson, *A History of Foreign Words in English,* London (Routledge), 1935, 354 pp.

CHAPTER IV

A general perspective of Greek and Latin elements in English is offered by Roland Grubb Kent in his attractive little manual on *Language and Philology,* Boston, 1923; and also by Frederick Bodmer in Part IV of *The Loom of Language,* London (Allen and Unwin), 1943. Abundant material for study can also be gleaned from Carl Darling Buck, *A Dictionary of Selected Synonyms in the Principal Indo-European Languages,* Chicago University Press, 1949, xix+1515 pp. Joseph

Delcourt's *Essai sur la langue de Sir Thomas More d'après ses œuvres anglaises*, Paris, 1914, 471 pp., and F. Th. Visser's *A Syntax of the English Language of St Thomas More*, Louvain, 1946–56, 956 pp., are highly specialized monographs on More's English. The most comprehensive work on Shakespeare's English is that by Wilhelm Franz: *Die Sprache Shakespeares in Vers und Prosa*, Halle (Niemeyer), 1939, 730 pp., this being the fourth edition of Franz's well-known *Shakespeare-Grammatik*. Henry Bradley's succinct survey of *Shakespeare's English* comprises Chapter XXX of Volume II of *Shakespeare's England*, Oxford, 1916; and George Stuart Gordon's essay on *Shakespeare's English* forms S.P.E. tract No. 29, Oxford, 1928. Richard Foster Jones, *The Triumph of the English Language*, Oxford University Press, 1953, xii+ 340 pp., gives a detailed account of current views on the use of English from Caxton to the Restoration.

CHAPTER V

Raymond Wilson Chambers's essay *On the Continuity of English Prose from Alfred to More and his School* forms part of the Introduction to Nicholas Harpsfield's *Life of Sir Thomas More*, Early English Text Society, Oxford, 1932, 174 pp., and it has also been published separately. Tyndale's English has been scrutinized by Stanley Lawrence Greenslade in *The Work of William Tindale*, London and Glasgow, 1938, 222 pp., which contains a special chapter on *Tindale and the English Language* by Gavin Bone. The classical book on the rise of Standard English is still Lorenz Morsbach's *Über den Ursprung der neuenglischen Schriftsprache*, Heilbronn, 1888, x+188 pp., but its substance is well summarized in the opening chapters of Wyld's *A History of Modern Colloquial English*, mentioned above. The distinctive features of London English are described by Barbara Alida Mackenzie in *The Early London Dialect*, Oxford, 1928, 152 pp., and local documents have been edited with introduction and commentaries by R. W. Chambers and Marjorie Daunt in *A Book of London English, 1384–1425*, London, 1931, 395 pp. The development of a mature prose style is well portrayed by George Philip Krapp in *The Rise of English Literary Prose*, New York (Holt), 1915, and by James Sutherland in his Alexander lectures *On English Prose*, Toronto University Press, 1957, viii+123 pp.

CHAPTER VI

Authoritative text-books on the sounds of English are *An Outline of English Phonetics* by Daniel Jones, Cambridge (Heffer), ninth edition, 1961, 378 pp., and *The Phonetics of English* by Ida Caroline Ward, Cambridge (Heffer), fourth edition 1945, 256 pp. The authors present their pictures from different angles. Jones has foreign students particularly in mind: Ward is more concerned with phoniatry and the rectification of faulty enunciation in the speech of British children. Both books contain lists of writings on phonetic theory, readers, vocabularies, dictionaries, wall charts, gramophone records, and other visual and oral aids. Among books on phonetic and phonemic theory the following may be specially commended: Maurice Grammont, *Traité de phonétique*, troisième édition revue, Paris (Delagrave), 1946, 492 pp.; Eugen Dieth, *Vademekum der Phonetik*, Berne (Francke), 1950, xv+452 pp.; Roe-Merrill Secrist Heffner, *General Phonetics*, Wisconsin University Press, 1949, 253 pp.; Charles Francis Hockett, *A Manual of Phonology*, Baltimore (Waverly Press), 1955, 251 pp.; and *Manual of Phonetics*, edited by Louise Kaiser, Amsterdam, 1957, xv+460 pp.

The Great Vowel Shift has been well described in the histories of English by Wyld, Baugh, McKnight, and Robinson; in Henry Sweet's *A History of English Sounds*, Oxford, 1888, 410 pp.; in Karl Luick's *Historische Grammatik der englischen Sprache*, Leipzig, 1914–40, xii+1048 pp., a great history unfortunately incomplete, covering phonology and the first part only of morphology (continued after Luick's death by his pupils Friedrich Wild and Herbert Koziol); in Otto Jespersen's *A Modern English Grammar on Historical Principles*, Part I, *Sounds and Spelling*, London (Allen and Unwin), 1909, xi+485 pp.; in Wilhelm Horn and Martin Lehnert's *Laut und Leben: Englische Lautgeschichte der neueren Zeit, 1400–1950*, Berlin (Deutscher Verlag der Wissenschaften), 1954, 1414 pp.; and in Eric John Dobson's *English Pronunciation, 1500–1700*, Oxford, xxiii+1078 pp.

An attractive book on *Runes*, containing excellent tables, maps, and photographs, has been written by Ralph W. V. Elliott, Manchester University Press, 1959, xvi+124 pp.

The evolution of the alphabet is portrayed in considerable detail by David Diringer in *The Alphabet, A Key to the History of Mankind*,

London (Hutchinson), 1948, xii+607 pp., a copious compilation, illustrated by photographs and diagrams. A more succinct presentation of the essential features is made by Ignace Jay Gelb in *A Study of Writing, The Foundations of Grammatology*, London (Routledge), 1952, xv+295 pp. The fullest exposition of the vital phase in the historical process is offered by Godfrey Rolles Driver in *Semitic Writing: From Pictograph to Alphabet*, Oxford University Press, revised edition 1954, 254 pp.

In *English Spelling, its Rules and Reasons*, New York, 1927, 115 pp., Sir William Craigie has prepared an erudite defence of our unphonetic orthography without special pleading. It may be usefully supplemented by Craigie's two S.P.E. Tracts on *Some Anomalies of Spelling*, No. 59, 1942, and *Problems of Spelling Reform*, No. 63, 1944. Henry Bradley's famous paper *On the Relations between Spoken and Written Language with special reference to English* was communicated to the International Historical Congress in 1913, printed in the sixth volume of the Proceedings of the British Academy in 1919, re-issued as a booklet by the Clarendon Press in the same year, and included in the *Collected Papers of Henry Bradley*, edited by Robert Bridges, Oxford, 1928. George Henry Vallins has made an excellent survey of the subject in *Spelling*, London (Deutsch), 1954, 198 pp., which includes a chapter on American spelling by John W. Clark of the University of Minnesota.

CHAPTER VII

The reader will find a systematic exposition of word-structure in Eugene Albert Nida, *Morphology, The Descriptive Analysis of Words*, Ann Arbor (University of Michigan Press), second edition 1949, 342 pp.; and a searching demonstration of word-analysis in Zellig Harris, *Methods in Structural Linguistics*, Chicago University Press, 1952, xv+384 pp. Part VI of Otto Jespersen's *A Modern English Grammar*, London (Allen and Unwin), 1946, 570 pp., is devoted to *Morphology* in the widest sense, including inflexion, affixation, and composition. A full and systematic account is supplied by Hans Marchand, *The Categories and Types of Present-Day English Word-Formation: A Synchronic-Diachronic Approach*, Wiesbaden (Harrassowitz), 1960, xx+379 pp.

Several readable books on words have appeared in recent years:

Ernest Weekley, *The Romance of Words*, London (Murray), 1912, 210 pp.; Owen Barfield, *History in English Words*, London (Faber), third edition 1954, 223 pp.; Bernard Groom, *A Short History of English Words*, London (Macmillan), 1934, viii+221 pp.; and J. A. Sheard, *The Words We Use*, London (Deutsch), 1954, 344 pp.; not to mention those well-known books on words by Stuart Chase, Vere Henry Collins, Ivor Brown, and Eric Partridge.

Skeat's ten 'canons for etymology', prescribed by him in the introduction to *An Etymological Dictionary of the English Language* (final edition 1910), are still generally valid. They may be compared with the principles laid down by Alan S. C. Ross in Chapter I of *Etymology*, London (Deutsch), 1958. In *Origins: A Short Etymological Dictionary of Modern English*, London (Routledge), third edition 1961, 998 pp., Eric Partridge has skilfully demonstrated the ultimate kinship of words now far separated in form and meaning. He has also added a supplement to Henry Cecil Wyld, *The Universal Dictionary of the English Language*, London (Routledge), revised edition 1960, xx+1450 pp. Word-lovers will frequently consult the great British and American dictionaries – *The Oxford English Dictionary* and Webster's *New International* – with all their supplements and abridgements.

CHAPTER VIII

John Grattan and Percival Gurrey present a straightforward analysis of sentences (according to word-classes) in *Our Living Language*, London (Nelson), 1925, 323 pp., whereas Otto Jespersen, in *Analytic Syntax*, London (Allen and Unwin), 1937, 170 pp., offers an entertaining display of linguistic algebra with multilingual illustrations. This book may well be studied in conjunction with those chapters in *The Philosophy of Grammar*, London (Allen and Unwin), 1924, 359 pp., which are concerned with 'ranks'. Five out of the seven volumes of Jespersen's *A Modern English Grammar on Historical Principles* are devoted to syntax.

More advanced views on 'structural analysis' have been put forward by Henry Allan Gleason in *An Introduction to Descriptive Linguistics*, New York (Holt), 1955, ix+389 pp. ; by Charles Francis Hockett in *A Course in Modern Linguistics*, New York (Macmillan), 1958, xi+621 pp.; by Archibald Anderson Hill in *Introduction to Linguistic*

Structures: From Sound to Sentence in English, New York (Harcourt, Brace), 1958, xi+496 pp.; and by Winthrop Nelson Francis, *The Structure of American English*, New York (Ronald), 1958, 621 pp. Harold Whitehall's *Structural Essentials of English*, London (Longmans), 1958, vi+154 pp., is a valuable little text-book summarizing all that is best in that recent theory.

CHAPTER IX

Michel Bréal's *Essai de sémantique*, Paris (Hachette), 1897, 372 pp., has been translated into English by Mrs Henry Cust under the title *Semantics: Studies in the Science of Meaning*, New York, 1900, 408 pp. Many demonstrations of semantic change will be found in James Bradstreet Greenough and George Lyman Kittredge's *Words and their Ways in English Speech*, new edition with introduction by Simeon Potter, Boston (Beacon Press), 1961, 460 pp. ; in George Harley McKnight's *English Words and their Background*, New York (Appleton-Century) 1923, 460 pp.; and in Chapter 8 of George Leslie Brook's *A History of the English Language*, mentioned above. *The Meaning of Meaning*, by Charles Kay Ogden and Ivor Armstrong Richards, London (Routledge), tenth edition 1949, xxiv+363 pp., is a provocative study, to which is appended a notable monograph on *The Problem of Meaning in Primitive Languages* by the well-known anthropologist, Bronislaw Malinowski (1884–1942). Gustav Stern's *Meaning and Change of Meaning with Special Reference to the English Language*, Göteborg, 1931, 470 pp., is a meticulous study, and it has evoked other such studies in Scandinavia, but the writings of Stern and his pupils are not easy to read, e.g. Arne Rudskoger, *Fair, Foul, Nice, Proper: A Contribution to the Study of Polysemy*, Stockholm (Almqvist and Wiksell), 1952, xi+505 pp. It is therefore all the more pleasing and profitable to turn to those books by Smith, Empson, and Lewis which apply semantic principles to literary criticism and interpretation: Logan Pearsall Smith, *Four Words: Romantic, Originality, Creative, Genius*, S.P.E. Tract No. 17, later reproduced as Chapter III of *Words and Idioms, Studies in the English Language*, London (Constable), 1925, 300 pp.; William Empson, *The Structure of Complex Words*, London (Chatto and Windus), 1951, 450 pp.; and Clive Staples Lewis, *Studies in Words*, Cambridge University Press, 1960, vii + 240 pp. A full bibliography of semantic studies and a useful synopsis of present-day theories will be found in Stephen Ullmann, *Semantics: An Introduction to the Science of Meaning*, Oxford (Blackwell), 1962, 278 pp.

CHAPTER X

The first English dictionary appeared in 1604. It was a small volume of only 120 pages, the work of a schoolmaster named Robert Cawdrey. Its title was indeed significant: *A Table Alphabeticall, containing and teaching the true writing and understanding of hard usuall English words, borrowed from the Hebrew, Greeke, Latine, or French, etc.* The subsequent story of English lexicography has been well told by Mitford McLeod Mathews in *A Survey of English Dictionaries*, Oxford, 1933, 129 pp.; by De Witt Talmage Starnes and Gertrude Noyes in *The English Dictionary from Cawdrey to Johnson*, North Carolina and Oxford, 1946, ix + 300 pp.; and by James Root Hulbert in *Dictionaries British and American*, London (Deutsch), 1955, 107 pp. *The Oxford English Dictionary* is, to be precise, the title of the 1933 corrected reissue (in twelve volumes and one supplement) of *The New English Dictionary on Historical Principles* founded mainly on materials collected by the Philological Society, Oxford, 1884–1928, edited by James A. H. Murray, Henry Bradley, William Alexander Craigie, and Charles Talbut Onions. 'New' was felt by many to be ambiguous: *Murray's Dictionary* was, and is, the title often preferred. *The Shorter Oxford Dictionary*, edited by C. T. Onions, third edition, with revised addenda, Oxford, 1955, 2538 pp., is far more than an abridgement, since its assiduous compiler has been able 'to supplement the word-content of the original dictionary and its chronological evidence from the collections gathered by many hands during the last fifty years with a view to a grand supplement or an extensive revision of that work'. *The Concise Oxford Dictionary of Current English*, by H. W. and F. G. Fowler, was also re-issued in 1951 with revised addenda, pp. 1501–28, by E. McIntosh. *The Pocket* and *The Little Oxford Dictionaries* are yet smaller versions. Besides these one-volume Oxford dictionaries there are many others among which Chambers's, Collins's, Everyman's, Macmillan's, and Pitman's may perhaps be named.

American dictionaries resemble illustrated encyclopedias. *Webster's New International*, second edition unabridged, Springfield, Massachusetts, 1934, xcv+3210 pp., edited by W. A. Neilson and T. A. Knott, claims to 'utilize all the experiences and resources of more than one hundred years of genuine Webster dictionaries' and to 'interpret both past and present civilization'. It includes a wide range of scientific and technical terms which are often excluded from British dictionaries. *Webster's New World Dictionary* and *Webster's New Collegiate Dictionary* are abbreviated versions which are constantly being revised and brought up to date. *The New Century*, New York, 1938, 2796 pp., edited by H. G. Emery and K. G. Brewster, and *The New Standard*, New York, 1946, xl+2814 pp., edited by J. K. Funk and commonly called *Funk and Wagnalls*, are rightly named 'encyclopedic lexicons'.

Daniel Jones's *An English Pronouncing Dictionary*, London (Dent), eleventh edition 1956, xlv+538 pp., containing 58,000 words and names in International Phonetic Transcription, has established itself as the authority on pronunciation. Its American counterpart by J. S. Kenyon and T. A. Knott, 484 pp., was first published at Springfield, Massachusetts, in 1944, and has since appeared in revised form. Peter Mark Roget's *Thesaurus of English Words and Phrases*, 1852, has been revised and enlarged by his great-grandson, Samuel Romilly Roget, new edition, London, 1960. C. O. Sylvester Mawson's American version bears the title *International Thesaurus of English Words and Phrases*; 'a complete book of synonyms and antonyms founded upon and embodying Roget's original work with numerous additions and modernizations'. H. W. and F. G. Fowler's *The King's English*, third edition, Oxford, 1931, 383 pp., should be studied closely by all who aspire after an impeccable prose style. Some strictures may indeed seem austere and even captious, but they should be weighed and considered. Other analytical and censorious books are *The Handling of Words and Other Studies in Literary Psychology*, by 'Vernon Lee' (Violet Paget), London, 1923, ix+286 pp.; Robert Graves and Alan Hodge, *The Reader Over Your Shoulder*, second abridged edition, London (Cape), 1947, 221 pp.; Sir Alan Patrick Herbert, *What a Word!* London (Methuen), 1935, xi+286 pp.; Stuart Chase, *The Tyranny of Words*, sixth edition, London (Methuen), 1947, 275 pp.; and especially Sir Ernest Gowers, *The Complete Plain Words*, London

(Her Majesty's Stationery Office), 1954, 209 pp. The last book was written 'at the invitation of the Treasury as a contribution to what they were doing to improve official English'. It is intended 'primarily for those who use words as tools of their trade, in administration or business'. It may well be used in conjunction with that well-known book of reference, Henry Watson Fowler's *A Dictionary of Modern English Usage*, Oxford University Press, 1926, 742 pp., still unrivalled and indispensable. A useful supplement is provided by Eric Partridge in *Usage and Abusage*, London (Hamilton), fifth edition 1957, 390 pp.

Many helpful guides to good writing have appeared in recent years: George Philip Krapp, *A Comprehensive Guide to Good English*, Chicago (McNally), 1927, 726 pp.; Arthur Garfield Kennedy, *Current English*, Boston, 1935, 750 pp.; Sir Herbert Grierson, *Rhetoric and English Composition*, Edinburgh (Oliver and Boyd), 1944, 170 pp.; George Henry Vallins, *Good English*, London (Deutsch), 1951, 223 pp., and its supplements *Better English*, 1953, and *The Best English*, 1960; Eric Partridge, *English: A Course for Human Beings*, Winchester Publications, 1949, 540 pp.; Cleanth Brooks and Robert Penn Warren, *Fundamentals of Good Writing*, London (Dobson), 1952, 537 pp.; R. W. Bell, *Say What You Mean*, London (Allen and Unwin), 1954, 116 pp.; and John Kierzek and Walker Gibson, *The Macmillan Handbook of English*, New York, 1960, 510 pp.

CHAPTER XI

Informative essays on Standard English, Colloquialisms, Slang, Cant, Jargon, Vulgarisms, Solecisms, Idiom, and Dialect will be found in Eric Partridge's *Usage and Abusage* just mentioned. The same author's books on slang contain ample bibliographies: *Slang To-day and Yesterday*, 'with a short Historical Sketch, and Vocabularies of English, American, and Australian Slang', London, third edition 1950, 500 pp.; and *A Dictionary of Slang and Unconventional English*, London (Routledge), fifth edition 1960, 1360 pp.; together with its skilfully abridged version, *A Smaller Slang Dictionary*, London (Routledge), 1961, 214 pp. All that Wyld says about regional, social, and occupational dialects in *A Short History of English* and *A History of Modern*

7

Colloquial English is illuminating. Alexander John Ellis's *The Present English Dialects* forms Part V of his copious work *On Early English Pronunciation*, published for the Early English Text Society in 1889. Walter William Skeat's manual on *English Dialects from the Eighth Century to the Present Day*, Cambridge, 1911, 150 pp., gives a good general picture. The standard work is Joseph Wright's *An English Dialect Dictionary*, founded on the publications of the English Dialect Society, London and New York, 1898–1905, six volumes. *The English Dialect Grammar*, forming the appendix to the last volume, can be obtained separately: Oxford, 1905, 720 pp. Wright's earlier monograph on *The Dialect of Windhill in the West Riding*, Oxford, 1892, had already set a high standard for separate regional studies, among which special mention may here be made of Joseph Kjederqvist, *Pewsey*, 1903; Alexander Hargreaves, *Adlington, Lancashire*, 1904; Börje Brilioth, *Lorton, Cumberland*, 1913; George Cowling, *Hackness*, 1915; Percy Hide Reaney, *Penrith*, 1927; Walter Haigh, *Huddersfield*, 1928; Helge Kökeritz, *Suffolk*, 1932; Eugen Dieth, *Buchan*, 1932; Harold Orton, *Byers Green, South Durham*, 1933; J. E. Oxley, *Lindsey*, 1940; Paul Wettstein, *Chirnside, Berwick*, 1942; Bertil Widén, *Hilton and Melcombe Bingham, Dorset*, 1949. More recent dialect studies have been made in the University of Leeds and deposited in the Brotherton Library. A full account of plans for *A Linguistic Atlas of England* by Harold Orton will be found in the Louvain periodical *Orbis, Bulletin International de Documentation Linguistique*, Tome ix (1960), pp. 331–48. At the same time, plans for an investigation of Gaelic and Scots have been succinctly presented by Angus McIntosh in *An Introduction to a Survey of Scottish Dialects*, Edinburgh (Nelson), 1952, xii + 124 pp. The Journals of the Yorkshire, Lancashire, and Lakeland Dialect Societies provide good reading.

On the other side of the Atlantic, *The Linguistic Atlas of New England*, directed and edited by Hans Kurath and sponsored by the American Council of Learned Societies, Providence, Rhode Island, 1939–43, 734 maps, three volumes in six, comprises the first unit of the prospective *Linguistic Atlas of the United States and Canada*. It is accompanied by *A Handbook of the Linguistic Geography of New Zealand*, Providence, 1939, 240 pp., which expounds the aim and methods of the survey. *Dialect Notes* is the journal of the American Dialect Society, and *American Speech* often contains articles on dialect.

CHAPTER XII

The standard work on family names is Percy Hide Reaney, *A Dictionary of British Surnames*, London (Routledge), 1958, lix+ 366 pp., which contains a long and instructive Introduction. It completely supersedes the excellent books by Bardsley and Weekley, which, however, can still be consulted with profit by the specialist. Two learned dissertations on occupational surnames have been contributed to Lund Studies in English by Gustav Fransson, *Middle English Surnames of Occupation*, 1935; and by Bertil Thuresson, *Middle English Occupational Terms*, 1950. Elizabeth Gidley Withycombe's *The Oxford Dictionary of English Christian Names*, Oxford, 1945, xxxvi+ 136 pp., has a brief but informative Introduction. Ernest Weekley's *Jack and Jill*, London (Murray), 1939, xii+ 193 pp., and Eric Partridge's *Name this Child*, London (Methuen), third edition 1951, are also commendable.

Part I of the bipartite first volume of the English Place-Name Society's publications contains nine essays by seven different authors on various aspects of toponymy. The last of these, Sir Frank Stenton's *Personal Names in Place-Names*, pp. 165–89, forms a link between personal and local nomenclature. Part II, consisting of a glossary of *The Chief Elements used in English Place-Names* by Sir Allen Mawer, has now been completely superseded by *English Place-Name Elements* by Albert Hugh Smith, comprising Volumes XXV and XXVI of the Society's Publications, Cambridge, 1956, 817 pp. These two volumes provide the place-name investigator with an invaluable work of reference which should be used in conjunction with the quintessential introduction to *The Concise Oxford Dictionary of English Place-Names* by Eilert Ekwall, Oxford University Press, fourth edition 1960, li+ 546 pp. Ekwall's bibliography includes not only the leading books on the subject but also the principal sources from which the earliest evidence is derived. This evidence is also discussed on its historical and ethnic backgrounds by Reaney in *The Origin of English Place-Names*, London (Routledge), 1960, x+ 277 pp. The Publications of The English Place-Name Society (Cambridge University Press), 1924 onwards, will cover all forty counties. B. G. Charles's *Non-Celtic Place-Names in Wales*, London, 1938, xlvii+ 326 pp. is important for the Welsh counties bordering on Cheshire, Shropshire, Hereford, and Monmouth. Angus Macdonald's *The Place-Names of West Lothian*, Edinburgh, 1941, xl+179 pp., covers an area now outside England politically but linguistically within the boundaries of the old Northern dialect. The investigation of the place-names of Wales has been undertaken by Melville Richards at Liverpool University. Work on Scottish place-names has been well begun by the staff of the School of Scottish Studies with its pleasant seat in George Square, Edinburgh.

The English Hundred-Names have been examined by Olof Arngart, Lund, Vol. I, 1934; Vols. II and III, 1939; and *English River-Names* by Eilert Ekwall, Oxford, 1928, cii+488 pp. In the Proceedings of the International Congresses of Toponymy and Anthroponymy various aspects of name-study are considered on a world background. The International Committee of Onomastic Sciences is now affiliated to the Council for Philosophy and Humanistic Studies of Unesco. Its official bulletin is *Onoma* and it has its permanent seat at Louvain.

CHAPTER XIII

A leading authority on the historical development of United-States English is George Philip Krapp, *The English Language in America*, New York, 1925, 2 vols. In *The Beginnings of American English*, Chicago, 1931, ix+181 pp., Mitford McLeod Mathews reprints in convenient form some of the more notable criticisms made on this form of English in its early days. The first edition of Henry Louis Mencken's *The American Language, An Inquiry into the Development of English in the United States*, was issued in 1919; and the fourth edition, corrected, enlarged, and rewritten, 798 pp., appeared in 1936. *Supplement One*, 792 pp., followed in 1945; and *Supplement Two*, 848 pp., in 1948. Discursive, vivacious, and highly entertaining, Mencken's copious volumes are indispensable to students of American idiom. Kemp Malone's brief but valuable essay on Noah Webster, entitled *A Linguistic Patriot*, appeared appropriately in the opening number of *American Speech*, 1925, pp. 26–31. This journal, now published by the Columbia University Press, is the leading quarterly devoted to 'linguistic usage'. Its articles, notes, and reviews maintain a high standard. *A Dictionary of American English on Historical Principles*, edited by William Alexander Craigie and James Root Hulbert, Chicago, 1938–44, 4 volumes, may be regarded as the Transatlantic supplement to *The Oxford English Dictionary*. Mitford McLeod Mathews, *A Dictionary of Americanisms on Historical Principles*, Chicago and Oxford, 1951, xvi+1946 pp., is also comprehensive and reliable. Other notable dictionaries are concerned with slang and dialect: Lester V. Berry and Melvin Van Den Bark, *The American Thesaurus of Slang*, New York, third edition 1960, 1300 pp.; Harold Wentworth, *An American Dialect Dictionary*, New York, 1944, xv+747 pp. In *British and American English since 1900*, London (Dakers), 1951, x+341 pp., Eric Partridge and John W. Clark consider several aspects of these varieties of our language. Other descriptive accounts are given by Thomas Pyles in *Words and Ways of American English*, London (Melrose) 1954, 240 pp.; by L. M. Myers in *Guide to American English*, New York (Prentice-Hall), 1955, 446 pp.; and by Albert H. Marckwardt in *American English*, New York and Oxford, 1958, 194 pp.

CHAPTER XIV

Stimulating chapters on the future of English will be found in Partridge and Clark's *British and American English*, just mentioned; and shrewd observations on the defective mechanism of English may be found in Marckwardt's *Introduction to the English Language*, noted above under Chapter I. In *Newspaper Headlines, A Study in Linguistic Method*, London (Allen and Unwin), 1935, 263 pp., Heinrich Straumann examines telegraphese or 'block language', including that of advertisements, book-titles, chapter-headings, film-captions, and catalogues. No comprehensive account of the languages of the world has appeared in English. Mario Pei's *The World's Chief Languages*, formerly *Languages for War and Peace*, London (Allen and Unwin), third (first British) edition 1949, 664 pp., describes prominent features; but, as its title implies, it deals with 'chief languages' only. A simple picture of 'other people's languages' is given by Mario Pei in *All About Language*, London (The Bodley Head), 1956, 175 pp., and by Simeon Potter in Chapters 7 and 8 of *Language in the Modern World*, Harmondsworth (Penguin Books), second impression 1961, 221 pp. If, however, we seek a comprehensive treatise on this subject we must still go to Father Wilhelm Schmidt, *Die Sprachfamilien und Sprachenkreise der Erde*, Heidelberg (Winter), xvi+595 pp., with a separate atlas of 14 maps; or to Antoine Meillet and Marcel Cohen,

Les Langues du monde, Paris (Champion), nouvelle édition 1952, xlii+ 1296 pp., with 21 detachable maps in the end-pocket.

Since Ferdinand de Saussure imbued linguistics with a new spirit in his lectures, published posthumously at Lausanne in 1916 by his pupils Charles Bally and Albert Sechehaye under the title *Cours de linguistique générale*, several instructive and stimulating books on language have been written by Otto Jespersen, Edward Sapir, Henri Delacroix, Holger Pedersen, Joseph Vendryès, Karl Vossler, Leonard Bloomfield, Louis Herbert Gray, Edgar Howard Sturtevant, Walter Porzig, Bruno Snell, William James Entwistle, Ernst Otto, John Bissell Carroll, John Rupert Firth, Joshua Whatmough, Henry Allan Gleason, and Charles Francis Hockett. In some ways the most penetrating and original of all these books is Sapir's *Language, An Introduction to the Study of Speech*, New York (Harcourt, Brace), 1921, 258 pp., profound, thought-provoking, and eminently readable. The most influential of all these books, however, has been Bloomfield's *Language*, London (Allen and Unwin), 1933, 573 pp., to which Sturtevant modestly avers that his own *Introduction to Linguistic Science*, Yale and Oxford, 1947, 174 pp., is merely preliminary.

A classified list of books on the English language will be found in the General Introduction, pp. 24–49, to the first volume of *The Cambridge Bibliography of English Literature*, 1940, and in the Supplement (Vol. 5), 1957, pp. 8–36. Year by year new books are recorded in two useful publications: *Annual Bibliography of English Language and Literature*, edited by Henry Pettit and William White for the Modern Humanities Research Association; and *The Year's Work in English Studies*, edited by Beatrice White for the English Association, of which Chapter III is devoted to a survey, or series of reviews, of books on the English Language. *A Bibliography of Writings on the English Language from the beginning of printing to the end of 1922* has been compiled by Arthur Garfield Kennedy, Harvard and Yale, 1927, xvii+517 pp., as well as an abridgement entitled *A Concise Bibliography for Students of English*, Stanford and Oxford, third edition 1954, 170 pp. From the pages of *Research in Progress*, a biennial supplement to the June issue of the Publications of the Modern Language Association of America, we can readily ascertain what investigations are now being attempted or contemplated in the various branches of English studies.

INDEX

This index does not include words used as illustrative examples and it contains no references to the Bibliography

Some other Pelican
books are described on
the following pages